Living Faiths

Hinduism

Neera Vyas

Series Editor: Janet Dyson   **Consultant:** Robert Bowie

OXFORD
UNIVERSITY PRESS

OXFORD
UNIVERSITY PRESS

Great Clarendon Street, Oxford, OX2 6DP, United Kingdom

Oxford University Press is a department of the University of Oxford. It furthers the University's objective of excellence in research, scholarship, and education by publishing worldwide. Oxford is a registered trade mark of Oxford University Press in the UK and in certain other countries

British Library Cataloguing in Publication Data
Data available

ISBN: 978-0-19-912997-3

10 9 8 7

Paper used in the production of this book is a natural, recyclable product made from wood grown in sustainable forests. The manufacturing process conforms to the environmental regulations of the country of origin.

Printed in Great Britain by CPI Group (UK) Ltd., Croydon CR0 4YY

Acknowledgements

The publishers would like to thank the following for permissions to use their photographs:

Cover: Godong/Robert Harding/Rex Features; **p.8:** WireImage/Getty; **p.9t:** Tamas Gerencser | View Portfolio/Shutterstock; **p.9b:** Boobl/ Shutterstock; **p.10:** Ark Religion/Helene Rogers; **p.14l:** BioLife Pics/ Shutterstock; **p.14r:** Getty Images Europe; **p.15:** Cihan Demirok, CIDEPIX/Shutterstock; **p.16:** Dan Ionut Popescu/Shutterstock; **p.22t:** PiXXart/Shutterstock; **p.22l:** Time & Life Pictures/ Getty Images; **p.22r:** Leonid Plotkin/Alamy; **p.24–25:** Dinodia Photos/Alamy; **p.26:** Dinodia Photos/Alamy; **p.28:** With kind permission from the Mother Meera Foundation USA; **p.29:** www.vivekanandcollege.org; **p.30l:** shaunl/iStock; **p.30r:** Prapann stock photo/Shutterstock; **p.34:** Getty Images North America; **p.35:** Mary Evans/Sueddeutsche Zeitung Photo; **p.36:** JAGADEESH NV/epa/Corbis; **p.40:** Adina Tovy/Getty Images; **p.41:** Bonnie Kamin/Getty Images; **p.42l:** Ian Shaw/Alamy; **p.42ml:** Visage/Getty Images; **p.42mr:** Image Source/Getty Images; **p.42r:** John Warburton-Lee Photography/Alamy; **p.45:** Ajay Shrivastava/Shutterstock; **p.50:** Getty Images; **p.51:** Keystone Pictures USA/Alamy; **p.52:** Alvey & Towers Picture Library/Alamy; **p.53:** Simply Signs/Alamy; **p.58l:** Getty Images; **p.58r:** World History Archive/Alamy; **p.59t:** Christer Fredriksson/ Getty Images; **p.59b:** Dinodia Photos/Alamy; **p.60l:** Art Directors & TRIP/Alamy; **p.60r:** PHILIPPE PSAILA/SCIENCE PHOTO LIBRARY; **p.63t:** Simply Signs/Alamy; **p.63b:** Phillipe Psaila/Science Photo Library; **p.64:** Jim West/Alamy; **p.65t:** SEWA UK; **p.65b:** AFP/Getty Images; **p.68t:** Art Directors & TRIP/Alamy; **p.68b:** Neera Vyas-Adams; **p.72:** AFP/Getty Images; **p.73:** Dinodia Photos/Alamy; **p.74:** Myles Fisher for Inter Faith Network; **p.76t:** Neera Vyas-Adams; **p.76:** AFP/ Getty Images; All other photos by OUP

Illustrations: Gareth Clarke

From the author, Neera Vyas: Love and thanks to my dear and wise mum for answering phone calls at all times of the day (and night!) and helping me with all areas of the project. Also to my poor abandoned daughter, for patience and understanding way beyond most adults, let alone most six- year-olds!

OUP wishes to thank the Patani, Dave and Morris families for agreeing to take part in the case study films and to be photographed for this title. We would also like to thank Jay Lakhani of the Hindu Academy for reviewing this book.

We are grateful for permission to reprint extracts from the following copyright material:

The Bhagavad Gita translated from the Sanskrit by Sri Swami Sivananda (Divine Life Society, 1986), reprinted by permission of The Divine Life Society, Rishikesh, India.

Gandhi: In My Own Words selected by Richard Attenborough (Hodder & Stoughton, 2002), reprinted by permission of the the Navajivan Trust, Ahmedabad, India.

The Upanishads translated from the Sanskrit by Juan Mascaró (Penguin Classics, 1965), copyright © Juan Mascaró 1965, reprinted by permission of Penguin Books Ltd.

Sewa UK logo and mission statement, reprinted by permission of Sewa UK.

Although we have made every effort to trace and contact all copyright holders before publication this has not been possible in all cases. If notified, the publisher will rectify any errors or omissions at the earliest opportunity.

Links to third party websites are provided by Oxford in good faith and for information only. Oxford disclaims any responsibility for the materials contained in any third party website referenced in this work.

Contents

Introduction

What's it like to be a Hindu?

The *Living Faiths* series helps you to learn about religion by meeting some young people and their families in the UK. Through the case studies in this book you will find out first-hand how their faith affects the way they live and the moral and ethical decisions they make. The big question you will explore is: What does it *mean* to be a Hindu in twenty-first century Britain?

The icons indicate where you can actually hear and see young people sharing aspects of their daily lives through film, audio and music. This will help you to reflect on your own experiences, whether you belong to a religion or have a secular view of the world.

Key to icons

| Image gallery | Audio | Film | Worksheet | Interactive Activity |

The Student Book features

Starter activities get you thinking as soon as your lesson starts!

Activities are colour coded to identify three ways of exploring the rich diversity found within and between faiths. Through the questions and activities you will learn to:

- **think like a theologian**: these questions focus on understanding the nature of religious belief, its symbolism and spiritual significance
- **think like a philosopher**: these questions focus on analysing and debating ideas
- **think like a social scientist**: these questions focus on exploring and analysing why people do what they do and how belief affects action

You will be encouraged to think creatively and critically; to empathize, evaluate and respond to the views of others; to give reasons for your opinions and make connections; and draw conclusions.

Useful Words define the key terms, which appear in bold, to help you easily understand definitions. Meanings of words are also defined in the glossary.

Reflection

There will be time for you to reflect on what you've learned about the beliefs and practices of others and how they link to your own views.

Assessment

At the end of each chapter there is a final assessment task which helps you to show what you have learned.

Ways of helping you to assess your learning are part of every chapter:

- unit objectives set out what you will learn
- it's easy to see what standards you are aiming for using the 'I can' level statements
- you're encouraged to discuss and assess your own and each other's work
- you will feel confident in recognizing the next steps and how to improve.

We hope that you will enjoy reading and watching young people share their views, and that you will in turn gain the skills and knowledge to understand people with beliefs both similar to and different from your own.

Janet Dyson
(Series Editor)

Robert Bowie
(Series Consultant)

Meet the Families!

In this book, you will meet several young Hindu families from across the UK. You can read about their thoughts and views on various topics covered in the book, and also watch their full interviews on the *Hinduism Kerboodle*.

The Dave family

Neha and Nirav Dave live with their parents and grandmother in North London. Their cousin, Gaiatri, lives in North Wales. As a big, extended family, they celebrate some Hindu festivals together and meet for special family occasions. The Dave family particularly likes to share faith through music, song and dance!

The Patani family lives in Coventry. Nisha, her brother Niraj, and the rest of the family visit the Shree Krishna Temple regularly and the children both attend Gujarati school.

The Patani family

The Morris family

The twins Arian and Jay Morris live with their parents in Surrey. They are very close to their cousin Miran and his mother who live in the Midlands. Arian and Jay are examples of children being brought up as 'dual faith' — in their case, as Hindus and Christians.

Hinduism Faith Overview

To start at the beginning, Hinduism is so old that it cannot be given a start date – or even a founder! But there is evidence to suggest that people have been practising the Hindu faith in some form for at least 6000 years. What we know of as 'Hinduism' comes from a mixture of beliefs and customs practised by groups of people living and merging together in what is now India.

After Christianity and Islam, Hinduism is the third largest faith (going by numbers of people who call themselves 'Hindus'), both in Britain and across the world. There are about 900 million Hindus living in the world – and at least 600,000 Hindus in Britain.

Although most Hindus live in or originate from India, not all Hindus have Indian ancestry. For example, many Hindus in the UK are Europeans who have chosen to follow Hinduism. It's not right to say that these people 'converted' to Hinduism, because there is no real way of 'becoming' a Hindu – you either just follow the Hindu rules, called Sanatan Dharma (the 'Eternal Laws'), or not. There is no test to pass (like in Orthodox Judaism, for example), nor any special ceremony that demonstrates your commitment to the faith (such as baptism in Christianity).

Many other British Hindus have either come from India or have Indian ancestors, often via East Africa and some other places that were once part of the British Empire.

There also isn't one single Hindu sacred text or scripture to read and follow, like the Bible – there are various scriptures, such as the Vedas and the Bhagavad Gita, that Hindus

can consult. Important Hindu concepts that you will discover in this book include the ideas of ahimsa and karma, which is similar to the idea that you should treat others as you would like them to treat you. This concept is not laid down as an official 'rule', but it is the philosophy or thinking behind a lot of Hindu teachings.

The holy building where Hindus may go to pray is called a mandir or temple. However, many Hindus also worship at home, especially if there isn't a mandir nearby. At home, Hindus can worship at a home shrine, sing worship songs (known as bhajan) and make offerings to deities (known as daily puja). Hinduism also has many festivals, and one important one you may have heard of is called Divali, or the Festival of Lights, which is celebrated around October or November.

Overall, Hinduism is a complex faith, with no single set of beliefs or rules to follow. Some Hindus believe that there is One God, and others believe that there are many gods and goddesses. But you might ask: 'How can Hinduism have One God and a range of gods and goddesses?' To find out the answer to that and much more, read on!

1.1 Namaste! What is the Divine?

Learning Objectives

In this unit you will:

- develop understanding of some Hindu beliefs about **the Divine**
- use some theological vocabulary with confidence
- explore the meaning and significance of **atman** in Hinduism.

Starter

- How do you normally greet people? Why do you use those ways?

'Namaste' is a traditional Hindu greeting that can be understood to mean 'I bow to your **soul**'. Many Hindus believe that atman is the part of you that contains 'a spark of' the Divine. Saying and performing Namaste shows love and respect for both the Divine and also the person you are bowing to.

Useful Words

Atman The Hindu term for the eternal part of a person; many people use the term 'soul' to describe atman

The Divine The highest spirit beyond this world (God or gods/goddesses); most Hindus do speak about God (or gods), but saying 'the Divine' can be a more useful summary term

Soul The non-physical part of a person; many Hindus believe that it has a spiritual element

a Namaste is a traditional Hindu greeting where a person places their palms together and bows. It is now used more and more often by non-Hindus.

b

'The atman is said to be uncreated, not understandable and eternal.'
Bhagavad Gita 2.25

'Hidden in the heart of all beings is the Atman, the Spirit, the Self; smaller than the smallest atom, greater than the vastest space.'
Katha Upanishad, part 2

'He [or she] really sees, who sees the Supreme Spirit, existing equally in all beings.'
Bhagavad Gita 13.27

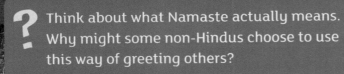

? Think about what Namaste actually means. Why might some non-Hindus choose to use this way of greeting others?

There are many different ideas about who or what God is in Hinduism, so the best way to sum it all up is to say that Hindus believe in **pluralism**. Belief in the Divine can take several forms. Some Hindus may also believe in more than one form. For example, many Hindus believe in *one* God who takes *many* forms (see Unit 1.2). Some feel strongly that this is a form of **monotheism**, while others would say it is **polytheism**. Others may see their beliefs as **pantheism**, because the 'many forms' include more than just gods and goddesses.

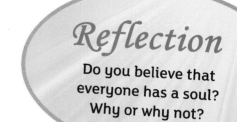

Reflection

Do you believe that everyone has a soul? Why or why not?

Pluralism is the concept that more than one form of the Divine (or idea about the Divine) can exist and be true at the same time. Plural means more than one.

Polytheism is belief in many gods and goddesses. Poly means many. For example, a polygon has many sides.

Atheism means an absence of belief in the Divine.

Monotheism is belief in only one God. Mono means one. For example, a monorail train runs on only one track.

Pantheism is the belief that the Divine is everywhere and everything is divine. Pan means all. For example, a panoramic view is where you can see everything – the whole picture. Many Hindus believe that the Divine can be everywhere at once and in all things – including all humans, hence saying 'Namaste'.

Activities

1. Look at the three quotations from Hindu sacred texts on the opposite page. Try rewording the quotations into your own words. Your aim is to show how these teachings may be used to encourage equality and respect for all.

2. Working alone, in pairs or in threes, demonstrate your understanding of some Hindu beliefs about the Divine. Create a mind-map that describes and explains the range of words and ideas from this unit. As well as words, you could use symbols, diagrams and pictures to show your learning.

3. Prepare your arguments for a debate about the statement: 'It doesn't matter if Hindus believe in monotheism, polytheism or pantheism, it's all the same thing really'.

Learning Objectives

In this unit you will:

- explore and analyse Hindu ideas about the Divine
- investigate the nature of some popular Hindu **deities**
- reflect on how believers connect to the Divine.

Starter

- Create a spider diagram to show all of the different roles you play. For example, sibling, friend, football player, etc.

Just as each of us is many different things at once, most Hindus believe that the Divine, often called **Bhagvan**, is also One *and* Many (see Unit 1.1). Many Hindus also believe that the Divine can take on a human or animal form at times, when the world needs extra guidance (see Unit 4.6). These forms are called **incarnations** or **avatars** (meaning 'in this body'). Most Hindus have a personal or family favourite image of Bhagvan.

Useful Words

Avatar/incarnation The Divine in human (or animal) form (the word avatar has also been used in recent years to mean an online image of a person)

Bhagvan A Hindu word for the Divine

Deity A god or goddess (the Divine)

? How does this image support the idea of 'One Supreme Spirit in many Forms'? Does the Vishvarupa image help you to understand this concept better, or does it confuse you?

a This image is called Vishvarupa. It symbolizes the idea of God as 'One Supreme Spirit in Many Forms'.

Case Study

Some young Hindus are asked to share what their favourite image of Bhagvan is and why.

Neha Dave, who is thirteen, particularly respects Lord Hanuman because 'every time anyone wants help, he would help them'. For Neha, different religions are just different ways of seeing one God: 'We have loads [of gods and goddesses], but it doesn't mean we don't believe in other ones, like Jesus. There is only one God, really.'

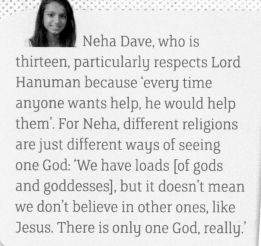

Neha appreciates Lord Hanuman's loyalty.

Gaiatri, Neha's cousin, who is only six, shares that she likes Lord Ganesha, 'because he is an elephant and I love elephants. He feels like my family.'

Nisha Patani, who is fourteen, identifies with the Divine in the avatar of Lord Krishna, because 'he has fun' and 'he's like one of us'. Even though many Hindu deities are portrayed as being 'strong, powerful and fierce', many are also thought to have a more 'human' side.

Lord Ganesha is also known as Ganapati.

Reflection

Does it matter what form believers imagine the Divine to take?

Activities

1. Design a symbol or explain in words suitable for a younger student, how 'one God can also be many'. Compare your outcomes with a partner or in threes. Which ideas work best and why?

2. Imagine that you have five minutes to interview Neha Dave about the issue of 'One Supreme Spirit in Many Forms'. Create a list of engaging questions to ask her that will help

you to learn more about her beliefs and how they affect her life.

3. Think about the statement 'The Divine cannot be fun'. How might Nisha Patani answer this? Work in pairs to script her likely response.

4. 'If God comes to earth to help out in times of need, why is there no incarnation right now? It's proof there is no God!' Prepare to argue your side in a debate about this issue.

1.3 Where are We Going? The Cycle of Life (and Death)

Learning Objectives

In this unit you will:

- examine links between Hindu lifestyles and beliefs about death
- reflect upon and begin to explain your own views about what death is
- evaluate the spiritual experiences of other people.

Starter

- Read the poem extract below from 'Do not stand at my grave and weep'. What does this extract say about death? Do you agree?

What death involves means different things to different people. Often this is shaped by their faith or cultural background, as well as their education and life experiences. Some firmly believe that death is the absolute end of existence and any form of consciousness. Others believe in some kind of **afterlife** – perhaps a 'perfect' place (such as heaven or paradise) or a terrible place (such as hell).

Hindu beliefs cover a range of views. There are concepts of temporary 'heaven' and 'hell', known as **swarg** and **narg**, and also a belief in returning as a 'spirit' or 'ghost' if the atman (the eternal part of a person) is too attached to a place or problem on Earth. However the main belief is **reincarnation**.

Useful Words

Afterlife Some kind of existence after death
Moksha Believed by many Hindus to be the ultimate goal of all souls: becoming one with the Supreme Spirit
Narg The Hindu term for hell
Reincarnation A cycle of birth, existence, death and rebirth
Swarg The Hindu term for heaven

a

'Do not stand at my grave and weep,
I am not there; I do not sleep.
I am a thousand winds that blow,
I am the diamond glints on snow,
Do not stand at my grave and cry,
I am not there; I did not die.'

Mary Frye

? What do you think is meant by the idea that the soul might be attached to a place on Earth?

12

For most Hindus, reincarnation means a cycle of birth, existence, death and rebirth. The soul – which is not physical – is believed to live many lives, each one being affected by actions in previous lives. The body is described in Hindu scripture as 'clothing' for the soul. When it is damaged or too old, the soul moves on to a new body – just as a person might discard worn out clothes and get new ones. Many Hindus believe that the aim for all souls should be to stop being reborn and to become one with the Supreme Spirit. This is called **moksha**.

b Look carefully at the picture for symbols as well as images that explain some beliefs about reincarnation.

'Just as a person casts off worn-out clothes and puts on new ones, the soul casts off worn-out bodies and enters others that are new.'
Bhagavad Gita 2.22

'For certain is death for the born and certain is birth for the dead.'
Bhagavad Gita 2.27

'At the end of many births the wise come to Me.'
Bhagavad Gita 7.19

'The soul may go to the womb of a mother and thus obtain a new body. It may even go into the trees or plants, according to its previous wisdom and work.'
Katha Upanishad Part 5

Some Hindus believe that *all* living things have a soul.

? How do these quotations support popular Hindu ideas about reincarnation?

Reflection

Can anyone ever know for certain what death means? Do you think that 'knowing' matters more than 'believing' something is true?

Activities

1 Demonstrate your understanding of at least one of the above quotations about reincarnation by putting it into a different format, e.g. a slogan, symbol, cartoon, or rap.

2 a What do you believe death means and why?

b How far are your beliefs about death shaped by family, friends or media, and how much is 'gut instinct' from you?

3 How might beliefs about death affect what you do in life? Discuss with a partner.

Learning Objectives

In this unit you will:

- develop thinking skills by reflecting on your place in the universe
- show understanding of different theories about time and existence
- identify similarities and differences between Hindu and other religious views.

Think about a starry sky and the vastness of space. The number of stars is mind-blowing and always changing. Every day – out there somewhere – a star 'dies' and a new one is 'born'. So where do we fit in? Is our planet any more or less important than all of the others in the universe?

Many Hindus would say 'not really', because they view creation as an endless cycle. They regard Earth as one of many millions of possible worlds. However, an alternative viewpoint – held by many monotheists in particular – is that the Earth and humans have been created specifically and specially by God. Many Christians, for example, believe that humans are the purpose of creation, not just a part of it.

Useful Words

Cyclical time Time with many beginnings and many ends
Eternal Lasting forever, with no beginning or end
Infinite Endless or eternal
Linear time There is a point at which time began and a point when it will end

? Compare and contrast the ways in which many Hindus and Christians understand their place in the universe. Which do you most identify with? Why?

ⓐ

ⓑ

Hindu scripture describes time as **cyclical** and **eternal**. This means that there are many beginnings and ends to creation. In Hinduism there are many stories about how this particular universe came into being, but the bigger picture is of endless universes in an **infinite** cycle of growth, existence, decline, destruction, renewal, regrowth and so on.

c The infinity symbol is a good representation of cyclical time.

However, several other religious traditions describe the universe as **linear**, meaning that time has one clear beginning and end.

'Where do all these worlds come from? They come from space. All beings arise from space, and into space they return.'
Chandogya Upanishad 1.9.1

'The God of Creation, who was born from the fire of thought before the waters were [...]
The Goddess of Infinity, who is Life-Force and Nature [...] Where the sun comes from and returns to [...]
What is here is also there and what is there is also here.'
Katha Upanishad Part 4

'I am the mighty world-destroying Time, now engaged in destroying the worlds.'
Bhagavad Gita 11.32

d Linear time suggests that existence will eventually end.

Reflection

Are people more or less or as important as the sand and earth we walk upon? What about the other planets and stars around us?

Activities

1. In pairs or threes, consider the powerful quotations above, all of which have been taken from Hindu sacred texts. Choose one and demonstrate your understanding of it by preparing each of the below:
   a A dramatic recital (including actions, pictures or props)
   b An explanation that unpacks the meaning
   c A summary of your group's agreement or disagreement about what is claimed.

2. Share your answer to the question 'What is Time?' as a piece of art, poetry or prose. Are there any problems with trying to depict time?

3. **a** Write a creation story of your own. It can be as imaginative as you like. (Remember that this task is about using your imagination and is not about specific creation theories based on evidence).
   b Share your story with a partner by reading it or acting it out.
   c Evaluate each other's accounts by considering the amount of effort put in, how interesting the account is, and what evidence there is of really thinking about the meaning of life. Also look at the quality of literacy.

1.5 Do You Know Your Place? The Caste System

Learning Objectives

In this unit you will:

- investigate the relationship between religious teaching and cultural practice
- compare Hindu ideas about **caste** with the way in which the class system affects life in the UK
- explore what caste and class might say about human nature.

Starter

- In groups, construct a spider diagram or list to answer the question: 'What roles does a society need to have so that it functions well?' For example, police officers, teachers, rubbish collectors, etc.

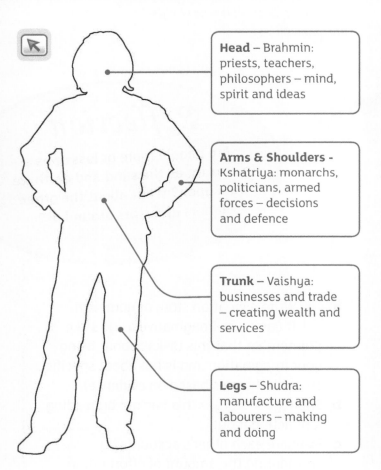

Head – Brahmin: priests, teachers, philosophers – mind, spirit and ideas

Arms & Shoulders - Kshatriya: monarchs, politicians, armed forces – decisions and defence

Trunk – Vaishya: businesses and trade – creating wealth and services

Legs – Shudra: manufacture and labourers – making and doing

a Many Hindus believe that the original purpose of varna was to have a well-ordered society, just as different parts of the body contribute to a person functioning at their best. However, over time, the caste to which a person belongs has become a matter of social status to some Hindus.

*'The fourfold varna has been created [...] according to the different **guna** and karma [actions] of people.'*
Bhagavad Gita 4.13

Varna (caste) is a system of social classes in Hindu culture. Many Hindus interpret the above quotation to mean that a person's varna should be based on their character and actions, and not on the family into which they happen to be born. They may also believe that varna divisions were useful in the past, but are not relevant in the modern world.

Mahatma Gandhi was passionately against varna, so he campaigned to reform the caste system in India (see Unit 3.1). He believed that varna limited life choices and encouraged people to think they are superior to others.

Useful Words

Caste A system of social classes in Hindu culture, based on the roles that people play in society
Guna The Hindu word for the (good and bad) qualities and characteristics of a person
Varna The Hindu word for caste

Case Study

Nisha Patani says 'I'm not expected to marry into the same caste, whereas in the past I would have been. But I would prefer to marry into the same caste, because the traditions would be the same.'

Nisha's view is common amongst many Hindus today, who believe that varna is not important other than as a shared cultural background.

Mrs Morris, who is married to a Christian, does not believe that 'the family or the caste you are born into should determine what job you do in the future or what chances you have'.

? Mrs Morris admires Mahatma Gandhi and agrees with his views about the caste system. However, some Hindus who also admire Gandhi still disagree with his views about the caste system. Why do you think this is?

Activities

1 Create a Venn diagram to show some of the similarities and differences between the Hindu caste system and the British class system.

2 Look back at your starter activity and make a pie chart of your responses, allocating portions of the pie depending on how important you think each area is. For example, if you think that emergency workers are twice as important as bankers, then the piece for emergency workers needs to be twice the size. What do your results tell you about what you believe matters in society? Compare your pie chart with the person sitting next to you. How similar or different are your results?

3 'People will always find something to pick on others for, so they can feel superior. If it's not their caste or class, it will be something like their hair colour or what sports team they support. It's just how most humans are!' Consider reasons for and against this statement.

Reflection

If all class and caste divisions were completely removed, would it make all of us the same?

Learning Objectives

In this unit you will:

- analyse and explain some ideas about the meaning and reality of truth
- interpret and respond to teachings about truth in faiths
- identify ways in which sharing faith may help social harmony.

Starter

- Discuss in pairs, what is truth? Is there only one definition of truth? (i.e. is 'I love you' true in the same way as '2+2=4' is?)

Many people believe that *their* view about an issue or a way of living is *the* truth. This can be the case for **atheists** as well as **theists**, including many Hindus. The main problem is that, when it comes to religious beliefs, there is no clear way of proving truth. While many Hindus are comfortable with this, and are open to respecting different beliefs (since most Hindus believe in **pluralism**), others find it difficult to tolerate other people's views.

Hindu scripture refers to 'truth' as 'everything that comes from the Supreme Spirit'. Because many Hindus believe that the Supreme Spirit is in everything, it could be said that they believe that 'everything is truth'. Mahatma Gandhi felt strongly about all faiths being equal, as the two quotes (to the right) from him show.

> 'This in truth is that, what is here is also there, and what is there is also here [...] those who see variety and not the unity wander on from death to death.'
> Katha Upanishad Part 4

> 'I know the beings of the past, the present and the future, but no one knows Me.'
> Bhagavad Gita 7.26

> 'Religions are different roads converging upon [meeting at] the same point. What does it matter that we take different roads so long as we reach the same goal?'
> Mahatma Gandhi

> 'The Bible is as much a book of religion with me as the Gita and the Qur'an.'
> Mahatma Gandhi

Case Study

Many people believe that teaching young people about a range of beliefs and moral issues in school is a good way of encouraging religious tolerance and social harmony.

 Neha Dave's cousin Gaiatri likes the way that everyone in her class has a chance to share their beliefs through the Collective Worship Book.

Useful Words

Atheist A person who does not believe in the existence of the Divine

Pluralism The concept that more than one belief about the Divine can be true at the same time

Theist A person who believes in the existence of the Divine

Case Study 🎞

Miran is eighteen and lives in Coventry with his parents. He believes that 'everyone has the choice to believe what they want to' and that we all 'should respect what everyone [else] believes in'. Miran feels 'accepted' by friends who have different beliefs to his own.

 Nisha Patani also lives in Coventry. She believes that 'we are all God's children' and that, together with her friends, 'we have learned to respect each other's religions'. Her brother Nirav agrees. He also has friends 'who don't believe in God whatsoever'.

? Coventry is a very multicultural city and has had a multifaith education programme for a long time. Do you think that this has had an impact on the views of these young people?

Reflection

Why do you think that most societies throughout history have had some kind of religious belief system? Is it just part of being human to need a 'higher power' to worship, blame and aspire to?

Activities

1 Does 'all paths' in the statement 'All paths lead to the Divine' include those who do not believe in the Divine? Spend one minute per person in groups of two or three deciding 'yes' or 'no' and give a reason.

2 Look back at the quotes from scripture and from Gandhi on the page opposite. Decide which one you find most interesting and use it to make a poster. Include words or pictures which explain what the quote means and what is interesting about it.

3 Prepare a lively article for a school magazine that examines whether teaching about different faith in schools is helpful to the personal, social, spiritual and moral growth of all young people, or if it's impossible to get across different beliefs fairly if they all claim to be about truth.

4 **a** Investigate the main principles of one of the following belief systems: Christian, Buddhist, Hindu, Humanist, Muslim, Jewish, Pagan, Rastafarian, Sikh.

b In pairs, compare your findings and consider how similar or different the main beliefs of the two faiths you and your partner explored are.

c Does your research lead you to agree or disagree with the statement that 'All paths lead to the Divine'?

Chapter 1 Assessment
What do Hindus Believe?

Objectives

- Explore and evaluate some key Hindu beliefs about the purpose of life
- Reflect on the meaning of life and justify an argument
- Develop effective presentation skills

Task

Use a range of presentation techniques to share your answers to the questions:

- What is the meaning of life, according to a Hindu?
- Do you agree or disagree with the Hindu view?

You must include reference to some Hindu ideas about the purpose of life, the Divine and atman.

A bit of guidance...

Aim to use a wide range of religious terms, and to give examples to support what you say. Don't be afraid to share your own views too (in fact, this is a key feature of progress in RE!) but do include reasons why you have those views in order to justify what you say.

Hints and tips

To help you tackle this task, you could:

- use ICT – PowerPoint, video clips, audio clips or sound effects, web links to newspaper accounts, for example
- create a background poster or use props
- have cue cards to support a PowerPoint presentation
- research an area that particularly interests you for further examples and evidence
- explore what some other faiths believe about the issue
- conduct a survey and present the results as a graph, and analyse the results as part of your evaluation.

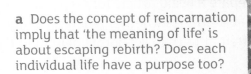

a Does the concept of reincarnation imply that 'the meaning of life' is about escaping rebirth? Does each individual life have a purpose too?

Guidance

What level are you aiming at? Have a look at the grid below to see what you need to do to achieve that level. What would you need to do to improve your work?

	I can...
Level 3	• use religious vocabulary to describe and evaluate some Hindu beliefs about the purpose of life and death • explore and explain my own view.
Level 4	• use a range of religious vocabulary to explain and evaluate some Hindu beliefs about the purpose of life and death • explore and explain my own view and some alternate views.
Level 5	• use a wide range of religious vocabulary to explore and evaluate a range of Hindu beliefs about the purpose of life and death • justify and evaluate my own view and a range of alternate views.
Level 6	• use religious and philosophical language accurately and with confidence to explore and evaluate a range of Hindu beliefs about the purpose of life and death • justify and evaluate my own view and a range of alternate views, with reference to how these views may impact individuals and society.

Ready for more?

When you have completed this task, you can also work on your skills for Levels 6 and 7, and perhaps even higher. This is an extension task.

In addition to Hindu views, your own reflections, and also some non-religious views (which are explored in the chapter), you could now go on to research, explain and evaluate responses to 'What is the meaning of life?' from at least one (ideally two) other faith or belief system. Include analysis of how these views impact on individuals and society. Finally, compare and contrast your findings with some of the Hindu views you have studied.

Learning Objectives

In this unit you will:

- learn about the origins of Hinduism
- investigate and analyse how symbols may be misinterpreted
- reflect on the idea that the meaning of symbols may change over time.

One of the most ancient Hindu symbols still used today is the **swastika**. The meanings and associations of this symbol vary. This variation has led to confusion for many non-Hindus and sometimes **prejudice** against Hindus, who have been mistakenly labelled as Nazis. This is because the Nazis chose the swastika as their symbol due to its links to the **Aryan** race, but for Hindus the swastika is a very old symbol for good luck. In fact, this symbol has been used by those who follow **Sanatan Dharma** (as well as many other groups) for thousands of years. What is now called Hinduism came about through the sharing, merging and writing down of beliefs from older traditions – including those of the Aryan race.

a A Hindu swastika

? How is the Hindu swastika similar to and different from the Nazi swastika? Which do you think came first? Does sharing a symbol mean that Hindus believe the same things as the Nazis? Give reasons for your answers.

b The Nazis chose the swastika as their symbol because Hitler and his followers idolized the tall, strong, highly intelligent qualities associated with the Aryan race. However, they may not have realized that the Aryans were part of the ancestry of modern Hinduism.

Unlike many other faiths, which are named after a person or concept (for example, 'Islam' means 'submission'), the term 'Hindu' actually comes from a place (the Indus Valley) in northern India. Early followers of Sanatan Dharma settled in this area and were called 'Hindus' by others in recognition of where they lived.

Another popular symbol of this ancient faith is the **Aum**. The Aum has many meanings. It is called the 'eternal sound' and the 'first sound', and features in some of the earliest Hindu sacred texts, such as the ones below.

? Can you draw the Aum symbol yourself?

'I will tell you the Word that all the Vedas glorify, all self-sacrifice expresses, all sacred studies and holy lives seek.
That word is Aum.'
Katha Upanishad part 2

'The atman [soul] is the eternal Word, Aum [...] The first sound A is the state of wakening consciousness [...] The second sound U is the second state of dreaming [...] The third sound M is the third state of sleeping [...]
The word Aum as one sound is the fourth state of supreme consciousness. It is beyond the senses and the end of evolution [...] it is love.'
Mundaka Upanishad

Reflection

Do you think that over time Hindus will be able to reclaim the swastika symbol, or is the Nazi legacy so great that this can never happen?

Activities

1. Draw both the swastika and the Aum, and label each with meanings and ideas associated with them.

2. Why do you think that the Nazis chose the swastika as their symbol? Write two paragraphs in answer to this question. Include your own ideas, as well as information from this unit, to help provide evidence for your answer.

3. Demonstrate your understanding of one meaning of Aum by creating a rhyme, rap, picture sequence or jigsaw puzzle which includes the different meanings and sections of this word.

4. Is 'Hinduism' a good name for this faith, or should it be called something else? What would an alternative name be based on and what would followers be called? Plan a list of suggestions and reasons for the names chosen.

Useful Words

Aum A symbol of Hinduism, meaning 'the eternal sound'
Aryan An ancient race from what is now India/Iran
Prejudice Making negative judgements about a person without knowing them; frequently based on something they cannot control, such as their race, gender or age
Sanatan Dharma This literally means 'eternal laws' and is the 'real' term for Hinduism
Swastika An ancient symbol associated with many groups; it means 'to be good'; it is used as a symbol of good luck in Hindu worship (the shape of the symbol represents good luck coming from the four corners of the world)

Learning Objectives

In this unit you will:

- recognize the diversity of sacred writing in Hinduism
- investigate some examples of scripture in Hinduism
- evaluate the relevance of ancient teachings to the modern world.

Starter

- Think of words from a favourite book (religious or otherwise), poem, or song that inspires you. Do these words affect the way you live? If so, how?

The age and evolution of Hinduism means that – unlike many other faiths – there is no single **sacred text**, nor even a small selection. There is instead a diverse collection of **scripture**, including myths, poetry, guidance and teachings.

Many Hindus have a particular favourite text, but others read from a range of holy books to suit particular occasions or situations. For example, followers of Lord Krishna may read from the Bhagavad Gita daily and a student might look to the Vedas for wisdom.

Hindu scripture mostly falls into two main categories or types:

- **Shruti** (meaning 'heard'). These are the oldest Hindu texts. They are believed to have been directly spoken to rishis (wise ones) and are seen as 'divine wisdom'.
- **Smriti** (meaning 'remembered'). These scriptures provide more structured guidelines for life, based on the 'divine wisdom'. They were originally passed through 'word of mouth' from guru to disciple (see Unit 2.4).

Useful Words

Moral About what is right and wrong
Sacred text Another name for a book that is considered to be holy and to contain divine wisdom
Scripture Writing; often used to refer to religious writing

Name of sacred text	Type	What it's about
Bhagavad Gita (the most popular part of the Mahabharata)	Smriti	God, in the form of Lord Krishna, gives the human Prince Arjun guidance and wisdom about the meaning of life during a battle
Mahabharata	Smriti	An account of the lives and adventures of the five Pandu Princes
Ramayana	Smriti	A poetic account of God's avatar (see Unit 1.2) as Prince Rama, including **moral** lessons
Upanishads	Shruti	Teachings about the nature of reality and moksha
Vedas	Shruti	A selection of prayers, hymns and rituals

Case Study

 Many Hindus have their own favourite sacred texts and stories. Neha and Nirav Dave like the Ramayana: 'We celebrate Divali because all the lights lit Rama and Sita's way back home'.

Nisha and Nirav Patani like 'a story from Krishna's life when his mother looked inside his mouth and saw the whole universe'. This is because 'you learn that Lord Krishna was God and at such a young age had the powers to make his mum forget what she saw'.

Nisha and Nirav like the story of the universe in Krishna's mouth because it shows that God understands what it means to be a 'normal' human child, despite also knowing the mysteries of the universe.

Reflection

'There's so much different scripture, from so many places, that it can't all be true. So it must be the case that none of it is!' Do you agree with this statement?

Activities

1. **a** Investigate one of the texts from this unit and compose a short blurb summarizing it for the back of its book cover.
   b Write a book review of it, including its key features, strengths and weaknesses.

2. Choose one of the stories, prayers, hymns or poems from the scripture you have studied and re-tell it in a format of your choice (e.g. a story book, cartoon strip, play, dance).

3. Imagine that you have to spend a year totally alone on an uninhabited island. All your basic needs are well met (food, shelter, clean water), but your entertainment options are limited to only three books.
   a Would you choose a sacred text or texts? If so, which one and why?
   b What other books would you choose to take and why?
   c With so many sacred texts to choose from (as well as all the other books published), do you think it would be more difficult for Hindus to make a choice than other people?

4. 'Hindu scripture is just so ancient and is all set in India, so it can't possibly have any relevance in twenty-first century Britain.' Prepare for a debate on this issue. Include examples and moral teachings from some of the texts to help support your case.

Learning Objectives

In this unit you will:

- learn that there are a number of languages associated with Hinduism
- evaluate whether meaning may be 'lost in translation'
- develop an understanding of how it feels to learn new languages.

Starter

- In the game Chinese Whispers, a message is whispered from person to person. By the end, the message has usually changed. Why do you think that is?

Shruti and Smriti wisdom (see Unit 2.2) was originally passed on by word of mouth. Gurus taught their followers the stories and **mantras**, which they had to learn off by heart. But, over time, people began to realize that using word of mouth could mean that meanings change, so it was decided that the wisdom should be written down.

The language of religion in Hinduism is Sanskrit, which although no longer spoken day-to-day, is the root of most Indian dialects. However, many Hindus today read scripture in the language they are educated in, which might be anything from English to Portuguese to Mandarin! Despite this, they may still learn some mantras in the original Sanskrit, or another language that is important to the culture of their family. One of the mantras that many Hindus from different backgrounds often recite in Sanskrit is the Gayatri Mantra.

Because of all the different translations of Hindu scripture, many Hindus believe that it is important to interpret texts intelligently, and to bear in mind that things can be lost in translation.

? Some accounts about scripture are so old that they are called 'myths' by many Hindus. For example, the Mahabharata is described as having been written down by Lord Ganesha himself. Do you think that Hindus who believe this would be more likely to follow the Mahabharata's teachings?

Case Study

For many Hindus, Nisha Patani included, connecting more with their ancestral (inherited) culture helps them to understand their faith better. Nisha's family originates from the state of Gujarat in north-west India. She has attended Gujarati School every Friday evening since she was six.

Nisha thinks that 'all young Hindus should learn about their language and culture', because 'some of the religious scripture is written in our language [Gujarati], so you need to learn the language so you understand the scripture better'.

Useful Words

Mantra A sacred phrase or prayer, usually chanted during worship or meditation

Reflection

Should there only be one global language that everyone is made to speak? You could present your reflections as an open book, with one page describing (in pictures or diagrams as well as words if you wish) reasons 'for' and the other reasons 'against'.

Activities

1 a In pairs, list at least three arguments to explain why organizations like Nisha's Gujarati School might be considered to be helping to enrich faith and culture.

b Using a different colour, add in counter-arguments (including any ways in which these organizations might be thought to divide society).

2 Do you think that learning a language with totally different letters and script to English makes it harder for young British Hindus to keep up with their traditional language(s) than for a person with French or German ancestors? Compose a social networking post (no more than 140 characters) to answer this question.

3 Look back at the account of how the Mahabharata may have been first written down. Does it matter whether Lord Ganesha really wrote down the Mahabharata? Is the source (where it's from) more important, or are the teachings? Share your thoughts with a partner.

4 What spoken wisdom (either from people you know or from yourself) would you choose to write down for generations to come? Think of something original, not just a common saying, and present it using creativity and care.

2.4 Who Guides the Way? Guidance from Gurus

Learning Objectives

In this unit you will:

- identify some qualities of a good spiritual leader
- investigate and evaluate the role and influence of **gurus** in the lives of some Hindus
- reflect on the qualities a guru should possess.

Starter

- Do you know what a guru is? List all of the words you can think of which relate to a guru.

The student stage is the first of the four main stages of life in Hinduism (collectively called **ashrama** – see Unit 5.3). Most Hindus today regard their normal education as their student stage, but some also choose to follow and learn from a religious teacher (often because their family follows this person). Others might discover a personal connection to a guru and their teachings, and choose to become their **disciple**.

Historically, most villages in India would have had at least one guru, who educated students both academically and spiritually. In the past, a person's guru was likely to be someone they knew, but today there are a whole host of gurus who interpret sacred teachings in the light of, and for the modern world. Many gurus share their thoughts using satellite TV, websites and stadium tours. However, individuals may still choose to regard someone they know and admire as their guru – the one whose wisdom they can learn from.

Useful Words

Ashrama The four main stages of life in Hinduism
Disciple A devoted follower
Guru The Sanskrit word for teacher or master
Mata Literally, 'mother', but also used as the term for female gurus
Swami A guru, usually male, who has entered the fourth ashrama (that of holy person)

? What do you think makes people follow Mother Meera and Swami Vivekanand? Try to think of a range of reasons to account for the followers of each person.

'One common mistake is to think that one reality is the reality. You must always be prepared to leave one reality for a greater one.'

'Like electricity, the Light is everywhere, but one must know how to activate it. I have come for that.'

a Meera **Mata** is believed by many of her followers to be an incarnation (human form) of Shakti (the female essence of God).

'Truth can be stated in a thousand different ways, yet each one can be true.'

'You cannot believe in God until you believe in yourself'.

'Condemn none: if you can stretch out a helping hand, do so. If you cannot, fold your hands, bless your brothers, and let them go their own way.'

?
- Why might Swami Vivekanand's ideas appeal to non-Hindus as well as Hindus?
- Do you agree with his views or not? Give reasons for your answer.

b Swami Vivekanand is one of the most popular Hindu gurus.

'The syllable gu means shadows
The syllable ru, he who banishes them,
Because of the power to destroy darkness
the guru is thus named.'
Advayataraka Upanishad 14–18, verse 5

?
- What does the quote suggest that a guru's role should be?
- How might a teacher 'destroy darkness' for their students?

Reflection

Do you have anyone who you consider to be a guru? If so, why? If you don't have anyone like this, what qualities would you look for in such a person? The person you choose does not need to be religious.

Activities

1. Use the information in this unit, plus your own thoughts about the issue, to create a mind-map entitled: 'Ways in which a guru may enlighten their disciples'.

2. In your view, why is it that historically, across all faiths and cultures, there have been more male spiritual leaders than female? Discuss this in pairs before writing a paragraph to explain your thoughts.

3. 'Having a guru as a guide stops you from seeing the world completely from your *own* perspective.' Consider responses that support and deny this statement, and then share your own views by composing a short conversation between two people with different viewpoints. This could be presented as a single script or as a series of texts or emails.

Learning Objectives

In this unit you will:

- explain some reasons why Hinduism does not have one set of rules or one leader
- explore the role of a Hindu priest
- reflect on how religious leaders can inspire people to follow them.

Starter

- Who are the people in the two pictures below? What do they have in common?

All of the main faiths (and most others too), apart from Hinduism, have a person or people who are the **religious founder** or founders of that faith. They represent the starting point of the faith – sometimes after their death (as with Jesus and Christianity), or during their lives (in the case of Muhammad and Islam).

Hinduism is different because there is no single founder or group of founders. Also, unlike most other faiths, Hinduism has many sacred texts rather than just one key book (like the Bible for Christians or the Qur'an for Muslims).

Useful Words

Mandir The proper term for a Hindu temple
Religious founder A person who is the starting point of a faith
Ritual An action or set of actions performed in a certain way, often as part of worship

a

b What do these two people have in common?

So, if there is no single book or individual to follow, how do Hindus know what the 'rules' are? The answer is that most Hindus will follow their own particular set of rules, based on a variety of sources that can include:

- their conscience (the bit inside us that tells us what's right and wrong)
- the teachings of any gurus who they might follow (see Unit 2.4)
- their own interpretation and understanding of the sacred texts
- their family's traditions and beliefs
- the advice and guidance of the priest at their **mandir**.

The Hindu priest's role is much like that of the local leaders in most faiths. He (although not forbidden, it is very unlikely to be a 'she') is usually responsible for worship and other events at the mandir, the celebration of festivals and rites of passage (key stages in life), and the giving of religious advice and education to the community – as well as setting a good example to other Hindus.

c Many faiths have local leaders.

Activities

1 Many Hindu priests have websites. What is your view about Hindu priests advertising their services? Is it the way forward, especially in the UK? Or does it seem wrong in some way? Give reasons for your views.

2 What do you think the most important part of a priest's duties are? Why?

3 In Hinduism there is no real religious restriction on women performing sacred **rituals**, but very few would call themselves a priestess. Why do you think this is? Discuss your ideas with a partner.

4 Discuss the following statement in groups of two or three, coming up with arguments for and against: 'There is no need for priests in a society where nearly everyone can read and interpret sacred teachings for themselves.'

Reflection

If someone started a new faith today, what do you think his or her message might be?

Where do Hindu Beliefs Come From?

Objectives

- Interpret and apply quotes from Hindu sacred texts and philosophers or Hindu leaders
- Develop and communicate your own point of view
- Evaluate evidence from a debate and make informed conclusions

Task

Draw on your learning about Hindu writings to debate the statement: 'The pen is mightier than the sword.' Do you agree or disagree, in light of your work on Hinduism? Explain your reasons.

a Prepare: In groups of four or five, identify and prepare quotations and examples to support each side of the argument.

b Debate: Use your quotations and examples to support what you say in a class debate about this issue. The debate could be held as a challenge – the 'Undecided' can sit in the middle. It's up to those with strong views to persuade the undecided to join them!

c Summarize: Use your preparation and ideas put forward during the debate to help you to produce a written (and visual if you wish) summary of the debate, including the pros and cons, and then your own judgment on which side is most convincing.

A bit of guidance...

You are aiming to show your understanding of some religious (and philosophical) writing, as well as giving your views and reasons. Don't just focus on what you think (and why), but also on finding and using appropriate quotations that you can explain and expand on as part of your evaluation and conclusion.

Hints and tips:

To help you tackle this task, you could:

- research different texts/websites during preparation time
- use examples from the news, TV and real life to support your views, as well as from a range of sacred texts.

Guidance

What level are you aiming at? Have a look at the grid below to see what you need to do to achieve that level. What would you need to do to improve your work?

I can...	
Level 3	• identify some relevant quotations and apply some examples from life or the media to support my response to the question • communicate my views clearly and include my reasons for those views.
Level 4	• identify and explain some relevant quotations and examples from life or the media to justify my response to the question • communicate my views effectively and include a range of reasons for those views.
Level 5	• identify, explain and evaluate some relevant quotations and examples from life or the media to justify my response to the question • communicate my views creatively and include a range of religious and philosophical reasons for those views.
Level 6	• explain, interpret and evaluate some relevant quotations and examples from life or the media to justify and illustrate my response to the question • communicate my views creatively and persuasively, including a wide range of religious and moral reasons for those views.

Ready for more?

When you have completed this task, you can also work on your skills for Levels 6 and 7, and perhaps even higher. This is an extension task.

'Most religions preach peace and practise violence.'

Reflect on this statement and use your understanding from the main task to write a short essay or speech (three or four paragraphs). Consider evidence for and against the statement before reaching a conclusion. To achieve a high level, you will need to justify your arguments by referring to at least two faiths, and relevant examples from life and the media.

Learning Objectives

In this unit you will:

- develop understanding about the concept of **karma**
- analyse the causes and purpose of suffering
- evaluate the purpose of Mahatma Gandhi's life
- consider what the purpose of your own life might be.

Starter

- Imagine how you might feel when:
  - however nice you are to her/him, your sibling seems to dislike you.
  - the new person in your class likes exactly the same bands, books and TV shows as you.

Some people might believe that the starter examples happened because of fate. Many Hindus don't believe in fate, but rather that all actions have consequences, and that what goes around comes around. This idea is called **karma** (which also means actions). 'Good karma' leads to positive consequences, but 'bad karma' creates **karmic debt** (which might include some suffering to help make up for previous bad actions). Many Hindus believe that the purpose of life is to repay outstanding karmic debt and to avoid creating more.

Some Hindus interpret being wealthy as an indicator of having had a good past life. However, others might point out that good karma is believed to lead to happiness and **spiritual fulfilment**, which is not the same thing as being rich.

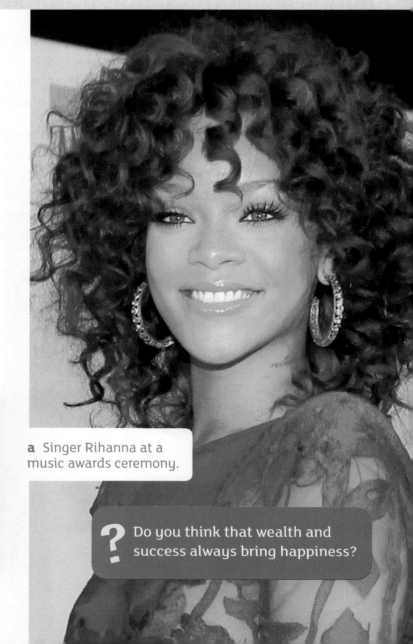

a Singer Rihanna at a music awards ceremony.

? In pairs or threes, discuss your responses to the two questions below, as well as the reasons for your views:
- What might a Hindu believe the good or bad karma to be behind the situations described in the Starter section?
- Do you agree or disagree with the idea that actions have consequences?

? Do you think that wealth and success always bring happiness?

The popular and respected Hindu leader Mohandas Gandhi was given the title Mahatma (meaning 'great soul'), because he showed an incredible amount of self-control and devotion to the Hindu principle of **ahimsa** (complete non-violence). He believed his purpose in life was to lead by example the message that all people are of equal worth and should be given equal respect and opportunity.

In order to fulfil this purpose, Gandhi was willing to go to prison and put his life at risk – both of which occurred several times. By being true to his beliefs, he inspired millions of others across the world to stand up for peace and equality.

Reflection

What do you believe the main purpose of your life to be? What leads you to this conclusion? How can you best achieve the purpose you have identified?

b Mahatma Gandhi – a man with a real sense of purpose!

Activities

1 Look at the photograph of the singer, Rihanna.
   a Make a spider diagram of the positive and negative aspects of wealth and fame.
   b Using a different colour, add in notes about what you think a Hindu might say in response to these issues.

2 Imagine that you are explaining what the Hindu concept of karmic debt is to five-year-olds. Use a range of strategies to share the concept in a way that they would understand.

3 Investigate the life and teachings of Mahatma Gandhi further.
   a Create a fact-file or presentation about him.
   b Share your findings with a partner and consider whether Gandhi is a good role model for young people today. Why or why not?

Learning Objectives

In this unit you will:

- identify and describe some popular Hindu festivals and rituals
- understand and explain the purpose of ritual in faiths
- explore why all humans seem to have rituals.

Starter

- Why do some sportspeople perform rituals such as doing a certain routine or meditating before competitions? How might they feel if they could not perform these actions?

Case Study

Neha and Nirav Dave perform daily **puja** and also take part in many Hindu celebrations throughout the year. Festivals such as **Raksha Bandhan** help them pause during their busy lives to reflect, celebrate, and give thanks.

Neha explains that Raksha Bandhan is important to her and Nirav because the rakhi (wrist band) 'protects him and makes the bond between a brother and sister stronger'.

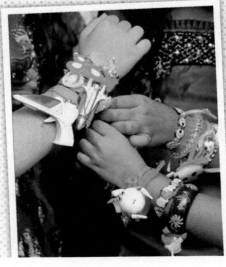

The ancient festival of Raksha Bandhan remains popular amongst many Hindus. Rakhi styles change over time and can be very up to date and modern.

The very unusual festival of Sitla Saatam originates in the fear of children dying from smallpox, which was quite common before vaccines were developed. Mothers would pray to the goddess Sitla Mata (literally 'the goddess of smallpox') to keep their young ones safe. Part of this appeal included a day when no fires were lit for cooking. Nowadays many Hindu families still keep this festival – not to prevent smallpox, but to maintain a tradition. It's something that brings their community together. Families and friends often get together and share cold food specially prepared the day before.

Case Study

Nisha and Nirav's favourite Hindu festival is **Janmashtami**. Nirav likes this celebration 'because you get to stay up late because he [Lord Krishna] was born at midnight.' Nisha enjoys being able to 'sing and dance with friends'.

Nisha and Nirav show their home shrine and explain what daily puja means to them.

'We believe we should take God's blessing before we take part in anything else. I feel more satisfied when I do puja at home.'

'When I take part in puja I feel relaxed and I also feel warm in the presence of God.'

Useful Words

Janmashtami A celebration of Lord Krishna's birthday
Puja Personal or communal (group) worship
Raksha Bandhan Literally a 'blessing bond', this is a festival where sisters give a rakhi (wrist band) to their brothers as a symbol of love and protection

Reflection

'Even non-religious people either take part in religious ceremonies at important times, or create their own "ritual" for an event, e.g. marriage. This proves that humans need to have rituals.' Do you agree?

Activities

1. If you could design a special festival, what would be the focus and what rituals would it involve? Why? Create a plan for 'My Festival' including when, why and how it will be celebrated.

2. Research the origins and rituals associated with some other Hindu festivals. Use the Internet and school library to help you find out the names, events and meanings of at least one other Hindu celebration.

3. Statement 1: 'Even if something is a religious ritual, we should question it and use our logic, not just do it!'
Statement 2: 'It doesn't really matter what the ritual is for – it's about bringing people together and having a sense of tradition.'
Compose a speech or blog to support one of the above views. Include reasons for your choice.

A Family Affair

Learning Objectives

In this unit you will:

- recognize the importance of family in Hinduism
- learn that, for many Hindus, participating in faith events is a way of learning
- reflect on some Hindu beliefs about life and death.

- When and why do families get together? Share ideas in twos and threes, and construct a spider diagram which summarizes your responses.

The answer that many Hindus would give to the Starter question is: 'as often as possible and for any reason!' Family is an essential feature of faith and culture for most Hindus.

Here, some Hindu families share their feelings about how their faith and family go together.

The Morris family visit their **extended family**, including cousin Miran and his mother, for festivals.

Miran enjoys festivals, but emphasizes that 'every day should be a feast because it is really important in Hinduism. Our upbringing is to be very close to our families, so even if it is not a festival, we usually eat together every day anyway'.

Miran's mother describes how at Divali (a major Hindu festival) 'all our families get together and light candles, and we all bring along different types of food. We have made beautiful sweets and just eat and celebrate!'

Different generations of the extended Dave family enjoy getting together and learning from one another.

Neha and Nirav Dave like to hear family anecdotes and learn more about some of the stories and practices in Hinduism from older family members. Neha enjoys finding out things that 'you may not learn in textbooks.' Nirav values time with his wider family, because 'you only get to see them every now and then'. This is partly because the extended Dave family is over 50 people!

In addition to being enjoyable, family gatherings such as festival celebrations and **bhajan** provide an opportunity for young Hindus to participate in and explore different Hindu rituals and practices.

The reason why the Dave family held the bhajan in the photograph below was to commemorate (remember and honour) loved ones who had passed away. This might sound quite gloomy, but the focus of this was on celebrating lives and sharing the family's love of singing and dancing. The Hindu belief in reincarnation (see Unit 1.3) means that those who have died are believed to be 'still living' in a different way. Therefore, Hindus commemorate the person that was alive and the eternal part of a person (atman) that they believe still exists.

Useful Words

Bhajan The term for sacred songs and also for an event where such songs are sung

Extended family The wider family group, including aunts, uncles, cousins, and close friends

Reflection

Do you think that commemorating the dead with family makes it easier for people to deal with the death of loved ones? Share your reflections with a partner.

a Many young Hindus learn more about their religion by attending events such as bhajan.

Activities

1. Do those attending the Dave memorial bhajan appear to be particularly sad or upset? Imagine you were there. Compose a social networking post describing the atmosphere.

2. 'There is no point singing to or for loved ones who have died, because they cannot hear us.' Do you agree? Prepare evidence to support your response in a class debate.

3. Hold a hot-seat event with one person taking the role of a member of the Dave family. They should respond to the statement in Activity 2.

4. What are the positive and negative aspects of spending time with your family? Work in pairs to draw a bird and write pros on one wing and cons on the other wing. Overall, do you value or resent spending time with your family?

Learning Objectives

In this unit you will:

- reflect on the idea that 'love' has many meanings
- investigate different ways in which Hindus show love for the Divine
- identify some ways in which religious beliefs affect people's behaviour.

Starter

- Choose a love song and think about the lyrics. What does the songwriter mean by love? Do you agree?

Love is a word with many meanings. The ancient Greeks simplified the problem by having different words for different types of love, as the diagram below explains.

Hindu scripture describes love for the Divine taking many forms. Three of the main ways in which many Hindus express their love for the Divine are:

? Do you think there is one answer to the question: 'What is love?' Why or why not?

- **Bhakti** – devotion and ritual
- **Gnaan** – wisdom gained from scholarly research and meditation
- **Karma** – actions which benefit the world

Agape – love for the world and humanity; the kind of love that makes people give their time or money to helping strangers or preserving the Earth for future generations

Eros – romantic love

Philos – love for family and friends (pets could be included here too)

Storge – love for a place, activity or object, e.g. national pride, devotion to making music, being mad about cars

a The Shri Swaminarayan Mandir in Neasden, London.

All ways of showing love for the Divine are deemed equally valuable in the Bhagavad Gita, and many Hindus demonstrate their loyalty to the Divine in a range of ways. Different aspects of love appeal to different people.

- Bhakti inspires Hindus to create amazing art, architecture and music. They feel connected to the Divine in an intimate and awe-inspiring way.

- Gnaan requires a more academic approach to connecting with the Divine. The Bhagavad Gita states: 'Verily, there is no purifier in this world like knowledge. Those who are perfected in meditation, find it [ultimate knowledge of the Supreme Spirit] in time.' (Bhagavad Gita 4.38)

- Karma may appeal more to those who believe that 'actions speak louder than words'. Lord Buddha, who most Hindus regard as an incarnation (human form) of the Divine, is believed to have said: 'However many holy words you read, however many you speak, what good will they do you if you do not act upon them?'

b Devotion or bhakti can inspire Hindus to connect with the Divine through painting.

'The same am I to all beings; to me there is none hateful or dear; but those who worship me with devotion are part of me and I am also part of them.'
Bhagavad Gita 9.29

Reflection

'A loving heart is the truest wisdom.' What do you think this means? Do you agree?

Activities

1. Demonstrate your understanding of agape, eros, philos and storge by designing a symbol to represent each type of love.

2. Label your symbols from Activity 1 as 1, 2, 3, and 4 (in order of which type of love you think is most important) and add a sentence to explain your reasoning.

3. Now add at least one example (but ideally two or three where possible) of how each type of love affects your life. For example: 'I show agape by making charity donations. There is no romantic relationship in my life right now. My family are the most important thing in the world to me. I love chocolate/ rugby/singing/yellow etc., because…'.

4. Demonstrate your understanding of bhakti, gnaan and karma by:
   - *either* making a mind-map entitled 'Sacred Love' that details ways to express these three aspects of Hinduism
   - *or* creating a poster aimed at younger children that explains what bhakti, gnaan and karma are.

Learning Objectives

In this unit you will:

- develop an understanding of the Hindu belief in dharma (duty)
- evaluate the value of having set goals and duties in life
- reflect on your own place and role in the world.

Starter

- Create a 'life map' to show what you think the main stages of life are. Do you think that everyone has the same stages in their lives?

For many Hindus, the main aim in life is attaining moksha (see Unit 1.3). In order to do this, they need to fulfill the particular duties that they have during the stage of life (ashrama) they are in. This is called varnashrama dharma.

The four ashrama are (**1**) student (of life, not just academic study), (**2**) householder and parent, (**3**) retirement and sharing wisdom, and (**4**) sannyasin (giving up material possessions and concerns in devotion to the Divine).

Case Study

Nisha Patani has just finished Year 9 at school. For her, the student life stage (or ashrama) 'is not really a duty', because 'I enjoy learning new things and you don't have as many responsibilities' as in some of the later life stages. 'Having a sense of dharma [duty] motivates me and helps me to achieve what I want to.' Nisha believes that following dharma results in her behaviour being 'better than those without guidance in their lives, because there are certain things I'm not allowed to do'.

Case Study

Miran, who is currently at university, believes that the duty to learn applies 'throughout your life', and that 'it's not just in Hinduism.' Miran values the student life stage but, at the moment, he does not feel that being a householder and parent is for him – although he does appreciate that 'it's important that parents should teach their children about duties'.

Miran's aunt, Mrs Morris, is already living in the second life stage, because she has married and has children. Her view is that it's important to give her children good moral guidance and 'a balanced view'.

Reflection

'We all need a role in life.' Is this true in your view? If you agree, what is your purpose in life? If you don't agree, why not?

Activities

1. In pairs, interview each other for two minutes about whether having rules to follow may help to improve the behaviour of young people and whether it might restrict their freedom.

2. Create a spider diagram to show the different jobs that you do in all areas of life. Use a colour-coded key to highlight whether these different jobs are duties, leisure activities, or just a means to an end. Some of the jobs might have more than one colour that could apply to them.

3. Design a timeline of the four ashramas with words and pictures to describe each life stage.

Label the stages A (most) to D (least) according to how easy you think they are to fulfil.

4. 'The concept of varnashrama dharma makes young people better members of society.' In pairs, take on the roles of:
   - a Hindu who supports this statement
   - a Hindu who believes that varnashrama dharma limits their freedom and choices.

Conduct a debate in character, using evidence from the case studies and (ideally) additional research.

Learning Objectives

In this unit you will:

- identify the variety of ways in which Hindus may worship
- reflect upon what it means to Hindus to connect with the Divine
- identify and appreciate your own talents.

Starter

- Reflect: What does it mean to worship?
- Share: What ways of worshipping can you think of?

Case Study

Like Mrs Morris and her family, many Hindus perform daily puja (see Unit 3.2) as their main act of worship. However, there are also many other ways in which Hindus can express their devotion and love for the Divine. One of the most popular of these is singing bhajan (see Unit 3.3) and playing the instruments used for bhajan.

'We do our prayers in English, and we include 'Daddy', who is a Christian, as well. We ask for kindness and happiness and for peace across the world. Our worship consists of lighting small candles and then spreading the blessing across by remembering other people in the family.'

Nirav Dave loves to sing and play sacred songs. To be as good as Nirav at playing an instrument takes hours of practice, so his worship takes the form not only of bhajan but also of dedication to acquiring the skills to perform well.

'When I play the music I am more relaxed. It makes me feel much closer to God, because you are saying the words as if he is right there in front of you. I think it will carry on being part of my faith.'

Case Study

Hindus and non-Hindus alike use yoga as a form of exercise and mental relaxation. However for many people, performing yoga is not just about the mind and body but about the spirit too. Some Hindus may try to 'tune in' to the Divine during yoga. Here, Gaiatri is in a yoga position called the tree pose.

'I like to do yoga because it makes me feel happy. It makes me feel like I am worshipping.'

'Fix thy mind on me; be devoted to me; sacrifice for me; bow down to me; having thus united your whole self with me [...] you shall become part of me.'
Bhagavad Gita 9.34

? Many Hindus interpret this as meaning all actions devoted to the Divine or inspired by the Divine are acts of worship. Do you agree?

Many Hindus believe that doing your best to develop 'God given' talents (like sports, arts or science) is a way of worshipping the Divine too, because that's about appreciating what you are good at and using those talents to make the world a better place. In times when most people couldn't read or write, song and dance were an effective way of sharing sacred stories and worshipping. Even today, many young Hindus first come across tales and teachings through popular bhajan, or dances.

Reflection

Many people ask for help or gives thanks when in desperate need, or joy. Who or what are they appealing to? Why?

Activities

1. Try it for yourself! Try to copy Gaiatri's yoga pose – slowly breathe in through your nose as you move, and out slowly through your mouth as you come out of the pose. How did doing the pose feel? Do you think it is a spiritual activity, or do you think that yoga is just exercise? Share your views in pairs or threes.

2. Design your own mandala. Use repeated and complex patterns within a square or circular outline. Your mandala can be as colourful as you like!

a Many Hindus use a mandala to help focus their mind during worship. This is a very intricate and often geometric pattern designed to concentrate the brain when meditating.

Belonging to the Hindu Faith

Objectives

- Explore and explain some ways in which Hindus may express their spirituality
- Develop thinking skills by establishing connections between different practices
- Develop creativity and presentational skills

Task

Create a detailed mind-map of ways in which different expressions of the Hindu faith are connected, using the Dave family bhajan as your starting point. Use the questions below to help you plan your mind-map.

- Why did the Dave family gather on that occasion?
- How do the other Hindu families express their faith?
- In what ways might the younger members of the family: (a) participate in; and (b) learn about some aspects of Hinduism?

A bit of guidance...

Before putting the mind-map together, you need to gather and connect suitable information from your learning. This task is about attention to detail and really thinking. Once you have put a draft map together, look at it closely for any grammar issues and spelling errors. Also think about effective presentation techniques – use of colour and pictures, symbols or diagrams.

Hints and tips:

To help you tackle this task, you could:

- make two lists – ways in which some Hindus show their faith, and ways in which they learn about their faith; then colour code any areas which the young people have in common, e.g. Nirav Dave shows his faith by wearing a rakhi
- use your lists to help you to construct your mind-map
- add any additional information you have identified from this book, e.g. some Hindus study Sanskrit and other languages so that they can learn from Hindu scriptures.

Guidance

What level are you aiming at? Have a look at the grid below to see what you need to do to achieve that level. What would you need to do to improve your work?

I can...	
Level 3	• identify and connect ways in which some Hindus show and learn more about their faith • demonstrate my understanding in a clear and coherent way, using some religious vocabulary.
Level 4	• identify, explain and connect ways in which some Hindus show and learn more about their faith • demonstrate my understanding in a coherent and creative way, using appropriate religious vocabulary.
Level 5	• explain and connect a range of ways in which some Hindus show and learn more about their faith • demonstrate detailed understanding in a coherent and creative way, using religious vocabulary with confidence.
Level 6	• explain, explore and connect a wide range of ways in which some Hindus show and learn more about their faith • demonstrate detailed understanding in an articulate and creative way, using a range of religious vocabulary with confidence.

Ready for more?

When you have completed this task, you can also work on your skills for Levels 6 and 7, and perhaps even higher. This is an extension task.

Imagine that you have been put in charge of explaining to an alien what it means to belong to a faith. Using your mind-map, plan a presentation or booklet which explains what religion is, why so many people on Earth follow a religion, and different ways in which they show their faith. You must refer to examples from Hinduism and at least one other faith, and highlight some key similarities and differences between them. Your challenge is to get across some complex issues in an interesting and informative way.

Learning Objectives

In this unit you will:

- develop understanding of the aims in life held by many Hindus
- explore the dilemmas caused by artha
- consider the meaning of life and reflect on your ideas.

Starter

- Why do many people want to know what the meaning of life is? What do you think it is? Or do you think there is no meaning to life? Either way, consider the reasons for your views.

Many Hindus believe that there are four main aims in life, as set out in texts called Dharma Shashtras (books of law). These four aims are:

- **Dharma** – fulfilling personal, social and religious duty (see also Unit 3.5)
- **Artha** – earning wealth honestly
- **Kama** – achieving rightful desires of the senses through action
- **Moksha** – breaking free from the cycle of reincarnation (see also Unit 1.3)

Most Hindus believe that, of the three 'living' aims, dharma is the most important, and kama the least. This is largely because to achieve moksha, an atman needs to fulfil or complete their dharma.

It may seem unreligious to have 'earning wealth' as an aim in life. However, the Hindu concept of artha is about obtaining *honest* wealth. In religious terms, this means that making a fortune at the expense of someone else's happiness, or by exploiting the Earth's resources, would not be good karma. So it would not help to achieve a Hindu's ultimate aim of moksha.

a Making the most of the senses and seeking pleasure through art, music or pursuing hobbies is seen as a good thing in Hinduism (as long as it's not at the expense of dharma or causing harm to others).

In 2012, two of the five richest people on the *Sunday Times Rich List* (including the richest person in the UK) were originally from India and brought up in Hindu families. Both have set up and supported significant charity projects, but there has still been some controversy over how their wealth was obtained.

The biggest problem or dilemma when considering the aim of artha is how to define 'honest'. One person's definition of 'honest wealth' may not be the same as those of others.

Reflection

Does life only have one aim, or many, or none? Think about what leads you to your answer and give reasons for your response!

What is honestly earned wealth?

A Not breaking any laws in how it's earned.

B Making sure that *everyone* involved in the 'chain' is paid fairly.

C It does not involve causing pollution or using up valuable resources.

D Working hard and doing your best.

E It cannot involve exploiting other people or animals.

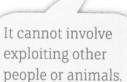

Activities

1 a List the four Hindu aims in life, including what each means, in order of which you think are the most and least important.
b Explain and justify your reasoning.

2 Select the view you *most* agree with from the five statements above. Prepare a one-minute sound bite that gets across why you think this is the most important aspect of 'earning wealth honestly'.

3 'Life has no meaning – we just happen to be here and can do what we like.'
a What kind of world would it be if everyone believed this? You could express your reflection as a collage, a poem, a series of photographs, or a piece of art/music.
b How positive or negative are your responses? Share your work in threes by creating an arts forum and taking on the role of art critics – discuss what each person's work says to you and why.

Learning Objectives

In this unit you will:

- develop understanding about what **ethical** decisions are
- explain how Hindus draw on their religion to find answers to ethical problems
- explore what influences you in making ethical decisions.

Starter

- 'Ending a human life, for any reason, is always wrong.' Think about your own response to this statement and why you feel that way.

Different Hindus will have varying responses to the difficult decisions we face. This is partly because there is a wide range of Hindu scripture that can be interpreted in different ways (see Units 2.2 and 2.3). The social and family values that a Hindu is exposed to also influence their views. Most people are affected by what has happened in their own lives and by the influence of education and media.

Useful Words

Ethics/ethical To do with right and wrong
Euthanasia Helping someone else to die

For many Hindus, issues of life and death often depend on whether they put the principle of ahimsa (see Unit 3.1) above other teachings and values. This is not straightforward, however.

a Tony Niklinson wanted his wife to help him die

The case of Tony Niklinson, pictured to the right, was covered recently in the media. Mr Niklinson was completely paralysed and could not move or communicate verbally for many years. He found it very painful to continue living because of his inability to move or speak, and he started a legal battle for the right to allow his wife to help him die (also known as **euthanasia**) without the risk of her being seen as a murderer.

Ahimsa teaches total non-violence, but it could be argued that it is more 'violent' to let someone suffer than to help them die painlessly.

Mahatma Gandhi (see Unit 3.1) is famous for his belief in ahimsa. He is a role model for many Hindus around the world.

'I see neither bravery nor sacrifice in destroying life or property for offence, or defence.'

'The sum total of all that lives is God. We may not be God but we are *of* God, even as a little drop of water is of the ocean.'

'I am an uncompromising opponent of violent methods, even to serve the noblest [most worthy] causes.'

'Birth and death are not two different states but different aspects of the same state.'

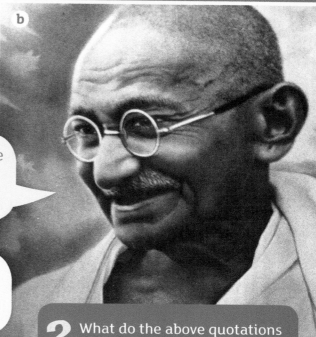

b

? What do the above quotations mean? Could any of them be interpreted as meaning 'killing in some situations is acceptable'?

Matters are complicated for many Hindus because one of the most popular sacred texts, the Bhagavad Gita, is actually set around the difficult decision that a prince has to make about whether fighting and killing his evil cousins for the throne is ethically acceptable. Prince Arjun is of the Kshatriya caste, so it is his dharma to protect the people of his kingdom. However, this goes against the teaching of no violent thoughts, words or deeds that is the basis of ahimsa!

Some of the advice that Prince Arjun is given by the Divine in the form of Lord Krishna is to the right.

'For certain is death for the born, and certain is birth for the dead; therefore, over the inevitable, you should not grieve.'
Bhagavad Gita 2.27

'But if you will not fight this righteous war, then having abandoned your own duty, you will have sinned.'
Bhagavad Gita 2.33

Activities

1. Imagine that Prince Arjun asks for *your* advice. What would you say he should do and why? Work in pairs and role-play the conversation, taking it in turns to be yourself and Prince Arjun.

2. Create a spider diagram showing the different teachings and beliefs that would be likely to affect a Hindu and non-Hindu's views on the case of Tony Niklinson.

3. Create a spider diagram showing what teachings or beliefs affect your own views about all the ethical issues raised.

4. Choose an ethical issue which most interests you and prepare arguments to speak for or against it.

Reflection

Can we ever really know what's right (or wrong)? Is it all just about how individual people see things, or is there such a thing as ethical truth?

Learning Objectives

In this unit you will:

- consider some of the difficulties involved in being a young Hindu in the UK today
- reflect upon your own **morality** – what really matters and why
- identify some links between Hindu teachings and morality.

Starter

- How do you know what's right and wrong? Where or who do you go to for advice?

A conflict between keeping a family commitment and hanging out with friends would present a really difficult **moral dilemma** for many young Hindus. It's not just a choice between 'philos' and 'eros' (see Unit 3.4), but also about their religious duty to honour their elders. It's part of dharma (duty in life) to show respect for parents and grandparents, so a young Hindu might feel that not going to the family celebration would not only be bad behaviour but also 'bad karma' (see Unit 3.1).

The same idea of karma also applies to some other everyday issues, such as what foods to eat, and whether we drive or walk. There might be a conflict between a person's desires and what the scriptures advise is good karma.

Useful Words

Morality A person's sense of right and wrong

Moral dilemma A situation where all of the options you face have something wrong about them – 'caught between a rock and a hard place'

? Identify how the two photographs in this unit could present moral dilemmas for young Hindus.

a

Sometimes, the dilemmas we struggle with have a much deeper impact on our lives. For many young Hindus, one of the greatest dilemmas in life is whether to still believe in the existence of the Divine despite the horrors of human cruelty (such as crimes and wars) and natural disasters. Their own reasoning or life experiences may cause them to have doubts about their faith.

Also, some of the ancient Hindu scriptures and rules which are less compatible with modern life may leave them feeling confused about what being a good Hindu really means. Therefore, many Hindus have to make difficult choices every day in deciding whether to follow advice from their faith, from the media, from family or friends, or simply based on what 'feels right'.

Reflection

Can we ever be really sure that our decisions are right (or wrong)? Share your reflections with a partner.

? It's your grandparents' anniversary celebration dinner, but on the same night your best friend invited you to their birthday party. You can't go to both. What do you do and why? What influenced your final decision? Was it:
- pleasing your family
- doing what your friends want you to do
- obeying a faith teaching
- following your heart
- working out what would be logically the 'best' thing
- or something else?

Activities

1. 'Is there a difference between religious rules and moral rules?'
   a Reflect on this question and then share your answer with a partner, giving at least one clear reason for your opinion.
   b In your pair, list what you think are the top ten rules that everyone should follow. Try to put them in the order of importance, with most important at the top, and least important at the bottom.
   c Label (or colour code) each one as 'religious', 'moral', or 'both'.

2. Is what's right and wrong always relative to the situation? For example, 'Murder is wrong, but killing in self-defence could be justified'. Or are some things always wrong? Share your thoughts as a diary entry or speech.

3. Some people believe that we are born knowing what's right and wrong, and that the sense of what is good and bad – shared by most people – is proof of a God who wants us to live in a certain way. Consider examples that support and deny this claim. Either present your thoughts as a 'For' and 'Against' table, or as a piece for a magazine.

4.4 Are You What You Eat?

Learning Objectives

In this unit you will:

- analyse some Hindu beliefs about diet and personality
- examine and explain why many Hindus are vegetarian
- examine what you eat and how it impacts your life.

Starters

- List what you have eaten in the last 24 hours. Is the food you have eaten good or bad for you, or somewhere in between?

Some Hindu scriptures give advice about how diet might affect a person's character and behaviour (and vice versa). In the Bhagavad Gita (17.8-11) there are three gunas (personalities) identified, each with certain types of food associated with them:

Useful Words

Fast/fasting To go without food, or some foods, for a period of time
Rajas/rajasic Passion/passionate or greedy
Sattva/sattvic Purity/pure
Sustainable Does not use all of something up; can be continued for a long time
Tamas/tamasic Lethargy/lethargic or lazy

'The foods which increase life, purity, strength, health [...] which are substantial and agreeable [filling but not hard to digest], are dear to **sattvic** [pure] people.'

'The foods that are bitter, sour, salty, very hot or too rich are liked by **rajasic** [passionate or greedy] people and result in pain or disease.'

'That which is stale, tasteless, rotten and impure [junk], is liked by the **tamasic** [lethargic or lazy people].'

Case Study

Here, members from the Dave, Joshi and Morris families discuss whether, and how, being a Hindu affects what they eat and drink. But it's not just about what they eat – many Hindus also **fast** on certain days or at certain times of the year. It's believed that the sacrifice of giving up some foods benefits mind, spirit and body.

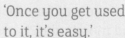
'Once you get used to it, it's easy.'

'Being a Hindu doesn't stop you from eating meat, but it's good to be a vegetarian. If you do eat meat, don't eat beef as it's a holy animal.'

Case Study

Miran explains that he eats meat but does not eat beef because it's 'killing a sacred animal [...] but apart from that, [eating meat] is down to personal choice, really'. Many Hindus agree with this view.

Miran's mother, who has been a vegetarian all her life, explains one of the reasons why cows are so special in Hindu philosophy: 'From the moment a child is born, cows provide milk for the baby, so why kill anything that gives us precious nutrition like that?' The cow also represents the mother figure.

'I do have a lot of special fasting days.'

Some Hindus decide whether to be vegetarian or to eat meat depending on how their caste groups ate in the past (see Unit 1.5). The ancient system was based on 'eat what you need':

- Brahmins and Vaishyas had mostly sedentary (sitting down) jobs, so they didn't need meat.
- Kshatriyas and Shudras had mostly active and physical jobs, so they needed the extra nourishment that meat provides.

Other Hindus are vegetarian because they believe that it is wrong to harm any living thing since they all have a bit of the Divine in them (see Unit 1.1).

Following a vegetarian diet is not always straightforward, as Aunt Joshi's sister (Mrs Morris) has experienced:

'When I used to travel with my job, I used to perceive myself as always being the awkward one but, as I grew older, my confidence grew and it never became an issue.'

Hindus who do eat meat may seek to eat meat that is **sustainable**, or from farms that treat animals well, so as to remain compassionate to animal lives.

Reflection

Do you agree with the statement: 'You are what you eat'? Share your thoughts in a personal blog.

Activities

1. Compose a rap, poem or limerick with the title: 'Reasons to be veggie'.

2. Some recent scientific research has suggested that fasting might help a person to have a longer and healthier life. If this were true, would it make Hindu teachings more or less valid and well founded? Discuss your thoughts with a partner.

3. Go back to your list of foods from the Starter. Identify which foods are sattvic, rajasic, or tamasic. Colour code them so that you can easily see which type you ate most of.

4. In pairs or threes, compare your results from Activity 3 and analyse whether they support or contradict the Hindu teachings about guna.

4.5 Special Feature
Food Glorious Food!

Learning Objectives

In this unit you will:

- make links between food and health
- develop understanding about the **Vedic** tradition of **Ayurveda**
- investigate the relevance of ancient wisdom in the modern world.

Starters

- What is medicine? Make a spider diagram containing all of the possible answers to this question.

The Vedas (see Unit 2.1) contain guidance about the whole of life, including how to have a healthy body, mind and spirit. This is called **Ayurveda** (literally 'life wisdom'). Early Hindu priests did not just perform religious rituals, but were also like doctors, giving advice about health matters.

Neha and Nirav Dave's great aunt follows Ayurveda to help her keep healthy and well. One of the main ways in which she does this is by using 'food as medicine' — not only in the sense of using some herbs and spices as treatments, but also by eating and cooking in ways that help to prevent problems in the first place.

Ayurveda is a way of life for many Hindus. Sometimes, without people even realizing, they are following it! For example, many of the ingredients in an authentic curry have been included because they are believed to improve health as well as flavour. But it's not just Hindus who appreciate **Ayurvedic** ideas — many of them are now being scientifically tested and recommended amongst non-Hindus.

Ayurveda is used by many Hindus for everyday problems. Look at the examples on the opposite page — they illustrate times when teenagers might find Ayurvedic remedies useful.

Useful Words

Ayurveda Ancient Vedic guidance on living well
Ayurvedic To do with Ayurveda
Vedic From the Hindu scriptures, the Vedas

a Neha's great aunt believes that 'food is medicine' and follows Ayurveda.

Ask Aunty Ayurveda!

Dear Aunty Ayurveda,

I have a really embarrassing problem – trapped wind! It's also painful – I get awful stomach cramps and sometimes can't sleep at night because of it. Please can you help?

Sharmila from Birmingham

Dear Sharmila,

Follow my advice and you will soon be free 'as the wind' and not trapped with it! You need to look at what, when and how you eat:

- *Don't eat fruit as pudding (eating fruits **before** meals avoids indigestion).*
- *Try not to drink anything with a meal. If you must, then drink before or during, but not straight after.*
- *Don't have hot drinks with, or just after, anything cold or acidic.*
- *Always sit down to eat or drink anything and really chew your food! Eating 'on the go' is a major cause of indigestion!*
- *Chew on a teaspoon of raw aniseed after a meal.*

Dear Aunty Ayurveda,

I have terrible spots and have tried remedies from the chemist, but nothing seems to work! Please can you recommend an Ayurvedic treatment that might help?

Savan from Norwich

Dear Savan,

You can have clearer and healthier skin in a few weeks! Firstly, flush out your system by drinking at least two litres of water every day. Mineral from a glass bottle is best, tap will do, but not flavoured or fizzy! Also, first thing each morning, drink a mug of hot water – this clears out toxins built up overnight.

Drink aloe juice each day and avoid junk and sugary foods. Eat plenty of fresh vegetables and fruit. Finally, use aloe gel on spots to calm and cleanse.

Reflection

'Remedies found in nature are proof that there is a loving and caring creator.' Consider this statement from a Hindu and secular viewpoint.

Activities

1. Would you try out the suggestions made by Aunty Ayurveda if you had similar problems? Give your response by writing a reply from either Savan or Rehana, either thanking Aunty and describing how they feel, or explaining why they think the advice did not work for them.

2. In pairs, imagine that you are asked to share views about Ayurveda in today's world. You can speak as yourself, as a Hindu who has grown up following Ayurveda, or as a new follower of Ayurveda.

The questions you need to answer (always with reasons and examples) are:

- Do you think that there is any health benefit in Ayurveda?
- Do you think that Hindus should try to embrace Ayurvedic traditions, or is Ayurveda just not relevant in the modern world?

3. 'Doing your best to keep healthy is a religious, social *and* moral duty.' How would Aunty Ayurveda answer this?

4.6 Animal Magic

Learning Objectives

In this unit you will:

- investigate how animals are treated by humans
- apply Hindu teachings to how animals are treated
- make informed decisions about issues to do with animals.

Starter

- Have you ever:
  - eaten meat
  - kept a pet
  - used an animal for transport?

Do you ever question whether or not it is acceptable to do the things in the Starter? How Hindus view animals is largely shaped by beliefs about what the Divine is and atman. For example, the Divine in the form of Lord Vishnu is believed to have had several animal avatars, as well as being a cowherd in the **avatar** as Lord Krishna. Most famously, the form of Lord Ganesha is beloved by many Hindus and attributed with the key qualities of wisdom and good luck.

Useful Words

Avatar Image or form

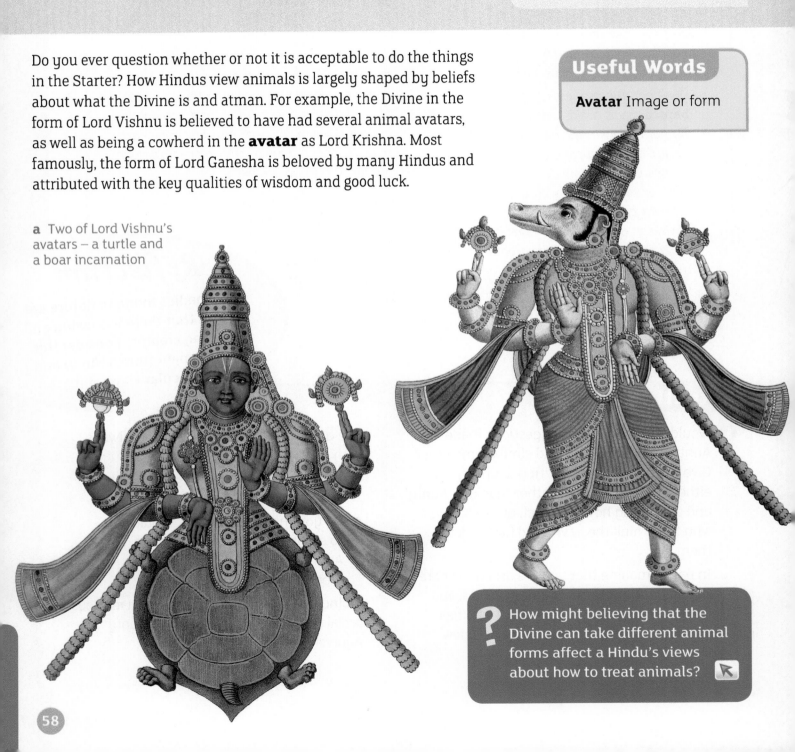

a Two of Lord Vishnu's avatars – a turtle and a boar incarnation

? How might believing that the Divine can take different animal forms affect a Hindu's views about how to treat animals?

Many Hindus also view animals as equal or sacred souls due to their belief in reincarnation (see also Unit 1.3). These views affect how most Hindus address issues about how humans use and care for animals.

b Many Hindus try to emulate (copy) Lord Krishna's care for cows.

? In what ways does the image of Lord Ganesha convey the Hindu idea that humans and animals are 'one'?

Reflection

Do you think that humans are more important than animals? Create a bird diagram with one wing for 'Yes' reasons and the other for 'No' reasons.

Activities

1. **a** Investigate Hindu views about one of the following issues:
    * Why cows are believed to be holy and how some Hindus express this
    * How some Hindus feel about animals being used to accompany and entertain humans
    * What Hindus believe about animal testing for the purposes of medical research
    b Use a range of communication skills to prepare an *informative* and *interesting* presentation to share your findings with a partner or group of three.
    c In your pairs or threes, evaluate each presentation on the quality of its research, content, communication skills and literacy. Give a mark out of ten for each area.

2. Plan a questionnaire that will help you to discover how people in your school and community view animals in terms of food. Consider the issues of animal welfare and the use of the whole animal if it's killed for meat (including things like the liver, brain and tongue). Also think about issues involving egg and milk production.

3. **a** 'A society can be judged by how it treats other living creatures.' Do you agree with this statement?
    b Can we only be held responsible for what we do individually, or is there a collective responsibility for how animals are viewed and treated by a society or culture?

4.7 Planet or People? Caring for the Environment

Learning Objectives

In this unit you will:

- examine some Hindu beliefs about the environment
- evaluate your own impact on the Earth's resources
- analyse the pros and cons of technological advancement.

Starter

- Does the Earth need humans or do humans need the Earth? Think and discuss with a partner.

Many Hindus believe that human beings need the Earth, and they pay respect to the Earth by worshipping the Divine in the form of Durga. Durga is known as the goddess of the Earth and the mother of the universe, and she uses her power to protect all life.

Just as the Divine tries to protect all life, including the natural world, many Hindus argue that humans should do the same as well. Actions such as littering and deforestation can have long-term consequences that affect both humans and the Earth.

> *'Nature's beauty is an art of God. Let us feel the touch of God's invisible hands in everything beautiful.'*
> Rig Veda 1.6.3

? What does the above quotation mean? How might God's involvement in creation impact on how a Hindu treats the environment?

a Durga, goddess of the Earth

b The devastating effects of deforestation leave a scar on the landscape.

Useful Words

Carbon footprint The environmental cost and consequences of how we live

Case Study

> As Hindus we believe that the Earth is our mother, so we should respect and look after our mother.

> I believe it is part of my duty to care for the Earth.

> It is our world; we are going to have to live in it, so why ruin it?

Like Nisha Patani, the Morris family believe in taking care of the Earth and reducing their **carbon footprint**. Mr and Mrs Morris share a concern for the welfare of the planet and how this may affect future generations, reflecting how well their Hindu and Christian backgrounds blend together. Mr Morris sees it as 'translating the duty and updating it for modern society'. His son, Arian, understands that 'We recycle our rubbish. We grow plants and walk to school.'

Jay and Arian Morris are being brought up to respect and care for the Earth with reference to both Hindu and Christian teachings about environmental responsibility.

Activities

1. Look at the picture of Durga. How does it support the idea that she uses her strength to take care of the Earth?

2. Make a list of all of the activities you do or participate in daily which could potentially harm the environment. Then, next to each activity, list some ways in which you could cut your personal carbon footprint.

3. 'It's a *moral* as well as religious duty for everyone to take care of the Earth for future generations.' Do you agree? Prepare a two-minute speech, or write an article for a school magazine, explaining *and* justifying your views.

4. 'Pollution is the price we pay for progress – is it a price worth paying?' Prepare arguments and evidence to support *both* 'yes' and 'no' responses to this question.

Reflection
What is your answer to the question in the title of this unit? Is it the planet that matters most, or people?

Raising Questions, Exploring Answers

Objectives

- Explore and evaluate in depth a moral issue from Hindu and other perspectives
- Use reasoning and evidence to inform your conclusions
- Explain a range of views as well as justify your own

Task

Your challenge is to produce an in-depth investigative news report into one of the moral issues featured in this chapter. Make sure that you include Hindu perspectives as well as your own point of view. Use different ways to present information, so that it's visually engaging and inviting to read, for example, graphs, maps, diagrams, speech bubbles, or information files.

A bit of guidance...

Choose an issue that you feel passionate about, would like to learn more about, or know something about already through school lessons or personal experience (e.g. euthanasia, or not eating meat). This will make your investigation more interesting and meaningful.

Hints and tips

To help you tackle this task, you could:

- plan how, where and when you will get your information
- try to include some primary evidence, such as conducting a survey and analysing the results, or interviewing someone involved in the area
- use secondary resources such as news reports, textbooks and websites intelligently
- construct your report so that there is an introduction explaining why you chose this topic and some key issues about it; present a range of views, including Hindu perspectives, and evaluate them; and finally, write a conclusion – which you should justify using examples and good reasoning.

Guidance

What level are you aiming at? Have a look at the grid below to see what you need to do to achieve that level. What would you need to do to improve your work?

	I can...
Level 3	• use research and communication skills to show my understanding about a moral issue • explain some Hindu responses to this issue • support my own views with examples and reasons.
Level 4	• use a range of research and communication skills to demonstrate my understanding about a moral issue • explain and evaluate some Hindu responses to this issue and explore at least one other view • support my own conclusions with examples and reasons
Level 5	• use an interesting range of research and communication skills to convey my understanding of a moral issue • explain, explore and evaluate some Hindu responses to this issue and at least one other view • support my own conclusions with a range of examples and reasons.
Level 6	• use a wide range of research and communication skills intelligently to convey my understanding of a moral issue • analyse and evaluate a range of Hindu responses to this issue and at least two other views • support my own conclusions with a range of effective examples and reasons.

Ready for more?

When you have completed this task, you can also work on your skills for Levels 6 and 7, and perhaps even higher. This is an extension task.

Demonstrate your learning by composing the script for a scene in a TV show or film, where your chosen issue is a point of conflict between at least two characters. Each character should be a member of a different belief system, including non-religious. Your aim is to get across the range of beliefs and explanations for them through what the characters say to each other.

Learning Objectives

In this unit you will:

- develop an understanding of the meaning of **sewa**, and also investigate the work of Sewa UK
- explore what motivates charity volunteers
- evaluate the value of sewa and Sewa UK in the modern world.

Starter

- Make a list of all the charities you know. Compare your list with others and add three more names.

Many Hindus interpret teachings like the two to the right to mean that it's their duty not only to support others but also to serve them. For instance, putting charity donations into a collection tin is relatively easy (although that doesn't mean you shouldn't do it!). However, to actually go out on the street and shake the tin, or go round gathering sponsors, takes more active involvement. That's real agape love! (See Unit 3.4.)

Some Hindus extend this sense of service to devoting a portion of their lives to serving others – either through regular voluntary work, or by taking part in a major project for several months or even years. Many Hindus find that they are able to show their sewa (duty to serve) by joining Sewa UK (a major Hindu charity).

'Perform your duty, for action is superior to inaction.'
Bhagavad Gita 3.8

'Whatever a great person does, others follow, whatever they set up as a standard, the whole world follows.'
Bhagavad Gita 3.21

? What makes people want to help others? What might motivate Hindus?

a Young volunteers show their sewa by helping to prepare meals for those in need.

Useful Words

Daya Compassion for all living things
Non-governmental Not linked to any political party or government
Non-sectarian All religions and beliefs (including atheism) are accepted
Sewa Service to others and the world

The charity Sewa UK makes it their mission to provide charitable aid to those in need. 'Sewa' means 'service' in the ancient Indian language of Sanskrit.

Sewa UK is committed to working in areas which suffer from disasters and tragedies. They provide immediate relief and rehabilitation by helping relief operations in the aftermath of such tragedies. They also provide support and care for the needy in the UK.

Sewa UK has members from all backgrounds and are a **non-sectarian** and **non-governmental** voluntary organisation registered with the Charity Commission for England and Wales.

? Research some of the projects that Sewa UK undertake, and discover more about the concept of sewa.

b Showing **daya** is an ancient duty that many Hindus still try to follow today.

'The person who is always involved in good deeds experiences incessant divine happiness.'
The Rig Veda

Reflection

Could you ever give up your time and money and leave your friends and family to help total strangers?

Activities

1 Create a spider diagram (with the title 'sewa') that includes reasons that explain why a Hindu would want to serve others. You could include references to the Hindu scriptures quoted in this unit, as well as the work of Sewa UK.

2 Add to your spider diagram from Activity 1 (in a different colour) some reasons why people who are not Hindus might also choose to serve others.

3 Does the reason why a person helps or donates to a charity matter, as long as the less fortunate benefit? Consider celebrities who want a 'caring profile'. Discuss your responses in pairs or threes.

5.2 What Shall I Do? Dharma and Career Choices

Learning Objectives

In this unit you will:

- expand your understanding of **dharma**
- analyse what makes a career fulfilling
- reflect upon your own and others' career aspirations.

Starter

- Do you know what you want to be when you grow up? What might influence your decision?

Most people want to follow a certain career path (either because they know something about that job, or because they want or need the money associated with it). This is also true for most Hindus. However, many Hindus also believe that it's important to consider whether they are fulfilling dharma through their work. They can consider this by asking themselves the following questions:

- Does it comply with artha (see Unit 4.1)?
- Does it encourage good karma (see Unit 3.1)?
- Does it comply with varnashrama dharma (see Unit 3.5)?

All of the above, along with other factors (such as peer or parental pressure, the qualifications required, and simply what the person themselves would *like* to do), means that choosing a career might be quite a problem for some Hindus!

For some Hindus, one factor might be more important than any other. For example, their family has 'always' gone into the armed forces, or been cooks, or (as many Hindu comedians joke) their parents really want them to be a doctor! Others may just aim to complete the student ashrama (see Unit 3.5) as well as they can and see where that leads them.

Useful Words

Dharma Duty; purpose in life

Case Study

The Morris twins would like to be an astronaut and an astrophysicist (or footballer) when they grow up!

Mr and Mrs Morris have not felt restricted in their career choices by their faiths. However, they say, 'collectively, our beliefs and our ethos did dictate that Mr Morris will take a job working for a charity'.

Case Study

Many of the jobs that these members of the Dave family do or want to do are fulfilling and make good use of their talents as well as being a way of earning money.

secondary school teacher

adult education assistant

caring for the elderly

voluntary work visiting sick people

architect or optician

dancer

pilot

Reflection

Are there any jobs that you could never do for moral or religious reasons?

Activities

1 Choose a person from the case studies and outline how they could fulfil dharma through their chosen career. Present your analysis as a mind-map, PowerPoint presentation or magazine-style feature. The questions below might help you complete this activity:
- Does the person's career choice encourage good karma? How?
- Would their faith make their job easier, more difficult, or would it have no impact? Give reasons.

2 a Produce a chart containing examples of jobs that you consider to be fulfilling or just careers
  b In pairs, compare your tables and share the reasons for your choices.

3 These days, most Hindus in the UK do not pursue careers associated with their varna (caste). Is this a sign of equality and progress, or is it a step away from their faith? Share your views by scripting or role-playing a conversation between a Hindu who *does* follow a career traditionally associated with their varna, and a Hindu who does not.

5.3 What about Relationships?

Learning Objectives

In this unit you will:

- develop an understanding of the connections between some ancient and modern Hindu beliefs and practices
- investigate and evaluate arranged marriage in Hinduism
- consider how Hindus might interpret scripture in different ways.

Loving relationships, marriage and family are very important to most Hindus. Many ancient texts and sculptures on Hindu temples reflect the importance of loving relationships. Hindu mythology includes many tales of gods and goddesses in love and some say that, at its heart, Hinduism is a celebration of **fertility** and creation. Teachings on relationships are interpreted in a range of ways by Hindus.

Useful Words

Fertility Ability to reproduce
Shaadi Hindi word for marriage

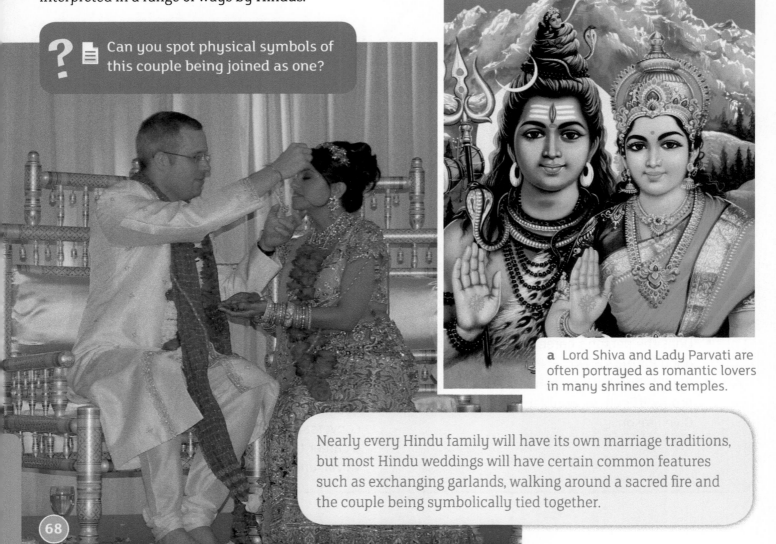

? 📄 Can you spot physical symbols of this couple being joined as one?

a Lord Shiva and Lady Parvati are often portrayed as romantic lovers in many shrines and temples.

Nearly every Hindu family will have its own marriage traditions, but most Hindu weddings will have certain common features such as exchanging garlands, walking around a sacred fire and the couple being symbolically tied together.

Many people associate arranged marriages with Hinduism. You may ask whether mutual attraction or romance between the bride and groom is considered when choosing a marriage partner, and the answer for most people today is 'yes'. For most Hindus in the UK, 'arranged' means an 'introduction', rather like a dating agency run by parents! For people from any background, consideration of how their families will get on is often an important feature of marriage – philos (love for family) matters as much as eros (romantic love) to most (see Unit 3.4).

> I'm open to suggestions - if there's anyone my parents have in mind, they should let me know, because I've got nothing to lose.

> I don't think arranged marriages work for me, I really want there to be a spark, and meeting a boy introduced by my family is always going to be a bit awkward.

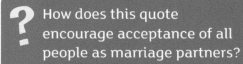

> 'In truth, it is not for the love of a husband that a husband is dear; but for the love of the Soul in the husband … It is not for the love of a wife that a wife is dear. But for the love of the Soul in the wife that a wife is dear.'
> The Brihad-Aranyaka Upanishad

? How does this quote encourage acceptance of all people as marriage partners?

> Marriage is not just about the man and the woman, it's also about linking our two families together, and I trust that my family will find the right husband (and new family) for me.

Activities

1. Read through the information about arranged marriages in this unit. Write a blog or diary from the point of view of a British Hindu who has either decided to join **shaadi**.com (a website used by some single Hindus to find a life partner), or to ask their family to help find them a partner.

2. What kind of questions do you think a British Hindu would consider most important to ask a potential partner? Think about what they would most value.

3. Consider whether you would trust your parents or guardians to find you a life partner. Discuss this in pairs giving reasons for your answers.

Learning Objectives

In this unit you will:

- evaluate the roles of women in Hindu culture
- identify and discuss differences between religious teaching and social practice
- explore and explain your own views about male and female roles.

There are many accounts of strong and wise female deities in Hindu scripture, and many Hindus regularly worship female forms of the Divine (see Unit 1.2). The central Hindu prayer, the Gayatri Mantra, refers to the supreme spirit as female (see Unit 2.3). The quotation below is from a set of sacred texts called the **Devi** Mahatmyam, which is all about **shakti** (female strength and energy). They describe goddesses who possess the ability to win against male enemies and competitors.

> 'The enemies began to strike her with swords in order to kill her. Devi Chandika very easily cut into pieces all the men and their weapons. Without any strain on her face, and with gods praising her, Shakti threw her own weapons at the bodies of the men.'
>
> Devi Mahatmyam 2.49

However, devotion to goddesses does not mean that there is no sexism in Hinduism. In common with many other cultures, Hinduism has a tradition of **patriarchy** – with men holding much of the power and often the finances too.

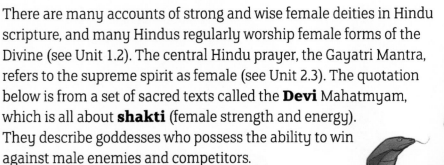

a The Shivashakti image demonstrates how many Hindu religious teachings emphasize gender equality.

? What do you think the Shivashakti image conveys about the status of men and women? Are there any similarities or differences highlighted?

Case Study

Three Hindu families share their views about gender issues in Hinduism.

> In the olden days, female roles were different. My grandmother would have to hold her sari over her face all the time while sweeping the floor!

> I don't think it matters whether you worship a female or male god, as long as you have faith. It just makes you stronger [...] Devi is the mother who is going to be there for you.

> Despite having had a relatively free youth, the older women in the Dave family had their career ambitions prevented because training away from home was 'just not done' in their day.
>
> Neha and Nirav's great aunt (age 75) believes that 'All the restrictions are passed by people. [Some men] think that they are at risk if they make us feel better than them!'

Reflection

'Gender inequality is very little to do with biology and everything to do with society'. Do you agree or disagree?

Activities

1. Create your own symbol, like the Shivashakti image, that shows the Hindu idea that male and female are 'one'.

2. Both Hindu and Christian wives traditionally take the name of their husband's family. In pairs, discuss why this is. Would you change your name or expect your partner to change their name, or not?

3. Bringing your thoughts together, *either* with a collage *or* a blog, titled: 'The Gender Divide is Down!' or 'The Gender Divide Remains!', depending on what your overall response is.

5.5 Militant Hinduism?

Learning Objectives

In this unit you will:

- examine and explain some of the areas of conflict between Hindus, and also between some Hindus and other groups
- evaluate some difficult issues about respect and tolerance.

Starter

- In what situations might a person feel the need to protest for religious reasons?

Most Hindus do not agree with a **militant** interpretation of Sanatan Dharma (see Unit 2.1). However, there are some small but active groups who believe that following Sanatan Dharma includes standing up for Hinduism – both against a more **secular** world and against other faiths.

Useful Words

Liberal Open to new ideas and willing to accept differences and changes

Militant Unwilling to tolerate the beliefs of others and willing to resort to violence

Secular Without religious reference; non-religious

This photograph shows some Hindus protesting against the Australian designer, Lisa Blue, who designed swimwear featuring the image of the Hindu Goddess Lakshmi. Images of Hindu deities can be found on a wide range of clothing, household goods (e.g. bags and stationery), and jewellery – much of which is made and sold by Hindus. However, the big problem in this instance is that 'skimpy' items of clothing (like swimwear) are viewed by some Hindus as disrespectful to Hinduism.

More **liberal** Hindus, on the other hand, might argue that – as the Divine is everywhere and in everything – it does not matter how images are used. These Hindus may also say that a more important issue is whether those involved in the manufacture and sale of items featuring Hindu deities receive a fair wage and have decent working conditions.

a Some Hindus protesting against the Australian designer Lisa Blue.

Even though most Hindus would agree with the quotations below from Mahatma Gandhi, other Hindus who hold more militant views can take their stance to extreme levels. In some areas of India, there continues to be intolerance of Muslims and Christians — despite this being against both the Hindu principle of ahimsa (non-violence) and the law of karma (good action).

> 'Intolerance is itself a form of violence and an obstacle to the growth of a true democratic spirit.'
>
> 'As soon as we lose the moral basis, we cease to be religious. There is no such thing as religions overriding morality.'
>
> Mahatma Gandhi

b Gandhi believed all people and religions are one.

Reflection

'The people who show religious prejudice would find something else to hate others for if religion didn't exist — it's about their character, not about the religion.' What do you think?

Activities

1. In pairs, imagine that you are British Hindu entrepreneurs who want to set up a young people's clothes and accessories store.

   a Role-play and then write a script for the discussion you might have when deciding whether to stock goods with images of Hindu deities on them.

   b To extend your thinking, consider other factors that might be of concern to Hindus and make a list of suitable questions. For example: 'Are the goods fair trade?' and 'Was child labour involved in their manufacture?'

2. Could one person ever properly represent *all* British Hindus on an issue? Explain how or why not in the form of a speech or letter to the press. Either:

   - appeal for support for *yourself* (taking on the role of a British Hindu who wants to represent all Hindus),
   - or speak as a British Hindu who does not wish to be represented by anyone else.

Learning Objectives

In this unit you will:

- evaluate the importance of **interfaith** activity
- identify ways people may learn from faith
- analyse your own and other people's reasons and actions in sharing beliefs.

Starter

- What is your response when you come across people giving out leaflets about their faith, or preaching (sharing teachings from their faith) in the street?

Hinduism is generally not an **evangelical** faith (see Unit 1.6). However, some Hindus believe that sharing their faith by inspiring and informing others is acceptable. They believe that there is no pressure to **convert** others, since Hinduism promotes pluralism, and the concept that the Divine is One *and* Many (see Unit 1.2). For example, the **mission** statement of the Hindu organization **ISKCON** says that Lord Krishna 'is the same God as The Father, Allah, Buddha and Jehovah'.

Most Hindus share their faith by how they live it. For example, through:

- festival celebrations
- food restrictions or fasts (see Unit 4.4)
- faith symbols included in their dress.

Useful Words

Convert To persuade someone to change their beliefs
Evangelism/evangelical Spreading a faith
Interfaith Between faiths
ISKCON International Society for Krishna Consciousness
Mission What a person or group aims for

a Many Hindus try to encourage peace between religions by taking part in interfaith groups, events and projects.

Case Study

Many Hindus share and demonstrate their Hindu beliefs and cultural connections in a variety of ways and to different degrees.

Miran prefers not to be 'open about [my faith] to all people, just to people I know'.

‑‑M‑ Gaiatri has chanted a sacred mantra and talked about her favourite deity form during Collective Worship at school.

Nisha Patani is happy to explain the symbolism associated with Hindu deities to people who ask: 'Why does this god have an elephant head?' or 'Why does this goddess have loads of arms?'

Many Hindus are happy to demonstrate and share their faith and culture in schools or community events, because this helps others to understand their way of life and builds a sense of community.

These families have made a commitment to sharing their faith with others in a variety of different ways.

Reflection

'There can only be ONE faith or NONE.' Do you agree?

Activities

1 **a** Create a mind map to include all the ways you can think of by which others can tell what you believe, and you can tell what they believe. (This can include secular and non-religious worldviews, as well as religious beliefs.)

b Add ways in which some Hindus might share their faith to your mind map (use *specific* examples).

2 Imagine that you have been invited to report on a Hindu celebration. Use all that you have learned in this unit to help you plan an account of your chosen celebration – focusing on how Hindus share their faith.

3 'Interfaith projects and events are just a waste of time; they all believe different things so trying to work together is no good.'

a Identify examples to support *and* deny this view.

b Create a response scale (from 1 – totally disagree to 10 – totally agree) which shows how far along your own view is.

c Explain and justify your position on the scale using your thinking from part **a**.

Objectives

- Demonstrate insight and understanding of some ways in which Hindus may respond to their beliefs
- Evaluate beliefs, commitments and the impact of some Hindus' views in the contemporary world
- Understand that although religious and cultural values are separate, they may be confused both by Hindus and others

Task

You are the Agony Aunt/Uncle for the new UK Teen website 'Young Hindu'. Because it's just launched, you've been asked to invent three letters to give readers a flavour of the kind of questions that they could email or text you about. You will have to provide answers as well as make up the problems!

A bit of guidance...

Sometimes Hindus may face a moral dilemma between what they believe their faith requires of them and the social norms. It may also be difficult for them to work answers out because they are influenced by culture, family, peers and the media.

Use the issues featured in this chapter, or any previous chapters, to help you come up with three really interesting and realistic problems that a young Hindu in the UK today may face. Your answers need to reflect an appreciation of Hindu teachings and (for higher levels) some of the diversity within the teachings and culture. You may also refer to moral values in your responses.

Hints and tips:

To help you tackle this task, you could:

- research further through news sites and the websites of Hindu groups in the UK
- apply previous learning to help you create a range of responses to the problems outlined in the letters – don't just tell the person what to do
- include some quotations from Hindu scripture or gurus in your responses.

Guidance
What level are you aiming at? Have a look at the grid below to see what you need to do to achieve that level. What would you need to do to improve your work?

	I can...
Level 3	• understand some problems that a young Hindu in Britain may face, and respond to them with sensible advice that includes Hindu teachings • identify features about religion and culture.
Level 4	• understand and empathize with some problems that a young Hindu in Britain may face, and respond to them with sensible advice that includes Hindu teachings and quotes • identify religious and cultural aspects of a problem.
Level 5	• appreciate and empathize with some problems that a young Hindu in Britain may face, and respond to them with a range of sensible advice that includes Hindu and moral teachings and quotations • comment on where there may be religious and cultural confusion.
Level 6	• appreciate the complexity of, and empathize with, some problems that a young Hindu in Britain may face, and respond to them with a range of mature advice that includes a range of Hindu and moral teachings and quotes • clarify where there may be religious and cultural confusion

Ready for more?

When you have completed this task, you can also work on your skills for Levels 6 and 7, and perhaps even higher. This is an extension task.

Either: Research and respond to the same problems from a secular perspective or that of another faith. Ensure that you refer to specific teachings or ideas.

Or: Tackle a more controversial issue as a Hindu Agony Aunt/Uncle, such as militantism or marriage.

Glossary

Afterlife Some kind of existence after death

Agape Love for the world and humanity

Ahimsa The Hindu principle of total non-violence in thoughts, words and actions

Artha Earning wealth honestly

Aryan An ancient race from what is now India/Iran

Ashrama The four main stages of life in Hinduism

Atheism An absence of belief in the Divine

Atheist A person who does not believe in the existence of the Divine

Atman The Hindu term for the eternal part of a person

Aum The symbol of Hinduism, meaning 'the eternal sound'

Avatar (incarnation) the Divine in human (or animal) form

Ayurveda Ancient Vedic guidance on living well

Ayurvedic To do with Ayurveda

Bhagvan A Hindu word for the Divine

Bhajan The term for sacred songs and also for an event where such songs are sung

Bhakti Devotion and ritual

Carbon footprint The environmental cost and consequences of how we live

Caste A system of social classes in Hindu culture, based on the roles that people play in society

Convert To persuade someone to change their beliefs

Cyclical time Time with many beginnings and many ends

Daya Compassion for all living things

Deity A god or goddess (the Divine)

Devi Hindu word for goddess

Dharma Duty; purpose in life

Disciple A devoted follower

The Divine The highest spirit beyond this world (God or gods/goddesses)

Eros Romantic love

Eternal Lasting forever, with no beginning or end

Ethics/ethical To do with right and wrong

Euthanasia Helping someone else to die

Evangelism/evangelical Spreading a faith

Extended family The wider family group, including aunts, uncles, cousins and close friends

Fast/fasting To go without food, or some foods, for a set period of time

Fertility The ability to reproduce

Gnaan Wisdom gained from scholarly research and meditation

Guna The Hindu word for the (good and bad) qualities and characteristics of a person

Guru The Sanskrit word for teacher or master

Infinite Endless or eternal

Interfaith Between faiths

ISKCON International Society for Krishna Consciousness

Janmashtami A celebration of Lord Krishna's birthday

Kama Achieving rightful desires of the senses through action

Karma The concept that your actions, and those of others, have consequences

Karmic debt The payment (in deeds or suffering) that is a consequence of bad karma

Liberal Open to new ideas and willing to accept differences and changes

Linear time There is a point at which time began and a point when it will end

Mandir The proper term for a Hindu temple

Mantra A sacred phrase or prayer, usually chanted during worship or meditation

Mata Literally, 'mother', but also used as the term for female gurus

Militant Unwilling to tolerate the beliefs of others and willing to resort to violence

Mission What a person or group aims for

Moksha Believed by many Hindus to be the ultimate goal of all souls; becoming one with the Supreme Spirit

Monotheism Belief in only one God

Moral About what is right and wrong

Moral dilemma A situation where all of the options you face have something wrong about them

Morality A person's sense of right and wrong

Narg The Hindu term for hell

Non-governmental Not linked to any political party or government

Non-sectarian All religions and beliefs (including atheism) are accepted

Pantheism Belief that the Divine is everywhere and everything is divine

Patriarchy A system where the father figure is in charge

Philos Love for family and friends

Pluralism More than one form of, or idea about, the Divine can exist and be true at the same time

Polytheism Belief in many gods and goddesses

Prejudice Making often-negative judgements about a person without knowing them

Puja Personal or communal (group) worship

Rajas/rajasic Passion/passionate or greedy

Raksha Bandhan A festival where sisters give a rakhi to their brothers as a symbol of love and protection

Reincarnation A cycle of birth, existence, death and rebirth

Religious founder A person who is the starting point of a faith

Ritual An action or set of actions performed in a certain way, often as part of worship

Sacred texts Another name for books that are considered to be holy and to contain divine wisdom

Sanatan Dharma This literally means 'eternal laws' and is the 'real' term for Hinduism

Sattva/sattvic Purity/pure

Scripture Writing; often used to refer to religious writing

Secular Without religious reference; non-religious

Sewa Service to others and the world

Shaadi Hindi word for Marriage

Shakti A word literally meaning 'strength' or 'energy'; also a term for the feminine aspects of the Divine

Shruti 'heard'; a term used for the oldest Hindu texts, believed to have been directly spoken to rishis (wise ones) and seen as 'divine wisdom'

Smriti 'remembered'; a term used for scriptures providing structured guidelines for life, based on the 'divine wisdom', and originally passed through 'word of mouth' from guru to disciple

Spiritual fulfilment Feeling complete, having a real purpose in life

Storge Love for a place, activity or object

Sustainable Does not use all of something up; can be continued for a long time

Swami A guru, usually male, who has entered the fourth ashrama (that of holy person)

Swarg The Hindu term for heaven

Swastika An ancient symbol associated with many groups; it is used as a symbol of good luck in many areas of Hindu worship

Tamas/tamasic Lethargy/lethargic or lazy

Theist A person who believes in the existence of the Divine

Varna The Hindu word for caste

Varnashrama dharma The duties that must be completed in order to attain moksha

Vedic From the Hindu scriptures, the Vedas

Index